Crisis Leadership in Higher Education

Crisis Leadership in Higher Education

Theory and Practice

RALPH A. GIGLIOTTI

Rutgers University Press

New Brunswick, Camden, and Newark, New Jersey, and London

Library of Congress Cataloging-in-Publication Data

Names: Gigliotti, Ralph A., author.
Title: Crisis leadership in higher education : theory and practice /
Ralph A. Gigliotti.
Description: New Brunswick : Rutgers University Press, [2019] |
Includes bibliographical references and index.
Identifiers: LCCN 2018059212 | ISBN 9781978801820
(paperback : alk. paper) | ISBN 978-1-9788-0183-7 (cloth)
Subjects: LCSH: Education, Higher—United States—Administration. |
Universities and colleges—United States—Administration. |
Crisis management—United States | Educational leadership—
United States. | Communication in higher education—United States.
Classification: LCC LB2341 .G486 2019 | DDC 378.1/01—dc23
LC record available at https://lccn.loc.gov/2018059212

A British Cataloging-in-Publication record for this book is
available from the British Library.

♾ The paper used in this publication meets the requirements of the
American National Standard for Information Sciences—Permanence of
Paper for Printed Library Materials, ANSI Z39.48-1992.

www.rutgersuniversitypress.org

Manufactured in the United States of America

To Mom and Dad for providing me with a strong values-centered foundation upon which to build a family and career

To Colleen for your enduring love, support, and encouragement

To Landon and Adeline for inspiring me every single day

Contents

Crisis Leadership in Higher Education

1

The Landscape of Crisis in Higher Education

Introduction and Context

Crisis is a prominent condition of contemporary organizational life (Roitman, 2014), and this is especially true for institutions of higher education. By their very nature, crises—which are growing in magnitude, frequency, and complexity (Helsloot, Boin, Jacobs, & Comfort, 2012)—have the potential to permanently tear at the fabric of an institution. The scenes of campus crises and their aftermath leave a lasting imprint on the minds, hearts, and legacies of many, whether it be the collapse of a newly constructed 950-ton pedestrian bridge at Florida International University, the rising floodwaters of the Iowa River and the collective efforts to fill sandbags outside of the Iowa Memorial Union at the University of Iowa, or the gathering of thousands of candle-holding students, staff, and members of the community at the iconic Rotunda on the campus of the University of Virginia days after a white nationalist march. These moments of disruption and discord in the life of an organization pose extensive challenges for the many impacted victims, yet they also serve as important communicative opportunities for the emergence of leadership (Fairhurst, 2007; Fairhurst & Sarr, 1996), sensemaking (Weick, 1979, 1995), and reflection (Barge, 2004; Barge & Fairhurst, 2008), and as a stimulus for organizational change, improvement, and renewal (Seeger, Ulmer, Novak, & Sellnow, 2005).

Crises are disorienting and unwieldy events for an organization and its leaders. These often senseless and complicated moments become crucible experiences for those with leadership responsibility. It is in the darkness and chaos of crisis where leadership becomes most critical, most visible, most desired. There is a well-established need for crisis prevention and management, as evidenced by the volume of books, training programs, and resources on the subject. At the same time, however, we are witness to countless cases of absent, ineffective, or counterproductive leadership in response to a wide range of crisis situations across institutions of higher education. The very uncertainty and unpredictability of these moments make the practice of crisis leadership that much more significant, complex, and critical. As college and university leaders wrestle with all that is required in the areas of crisis prevention, detection, management, and communication, these situations simultaneously provide a rich and compelling backdrop for the scholarly analysis of organizational leadership.

Leadership has become an increasingly popular topic in both scholarly literature and professional training and development (Ruben, 2012; Ruben & Gigliotti, 2016a, 2016b). As aptly noted by Fairhurst and Connaughton (2014a), "leadership is both new and old, a timeless concept that must simultaneously reflect the times yet stay ahead of them. To do so is no small feat, but it is most worthy of pursuit in contemporary organizational life" (p. 24). In many instances, the success or failure of an organization hinges upon the actions and decisions of those in leadership roles. More than a formal position or responsibility, however, leadership is understood to be a process of social influence that may be accomplished by any organizational actor. This process is shaped by verbal and nonverbal communication and co-constructed between leaders and followers, and by informal and formal leaders (Ruben, De Lisi, & Gigliotti, 2017; Ruben & Gigliotti, 2016). This conceptualization of leadership as a distributed and communicative process is especially relevant for the study of crises in higher education—situations that often demand a collective and collaborative response from multiple individuals, units, and organizations.

There was a time when "crises" on college and university campuses were relatively rare and episodic. When incidents did occur, they were usually contained within specific departments of a college or university. In addition, the management of such issues was largely the responsibility of the communication and media relations personnel within the institution. Much has changed, and at what seems like light speed. For example, I identified more than 1,000 recent articles from higher education news outlets, published between 2011 and 2015, that characterized some type of "crisis" in higher education. Rather than being isolated incidents requiring the sole attention of presidents, chancellors, or communication professionals, the proliferation of crises across campuses means that crisis leadership has now become fundamental to the work of university personnel across levels, disciplines, and institutions.

This book explores the nature of crisis in higher education—a context in which conflicts of various kinds across a diverse array of stakeholders are common, and where their occurrence often challenges core institutional values. The list of relatively recent examples of high-profile events in higher education that were labeled "crises" is overwhelming, and includes, but is not limited to, a sweeping college admissions bribery scandal impacting a number of prominent institutions; acts of violence triggered by white nationalist rallies at the University of Virginia; ISIS-inspired terrorist activity at Ohio State University; the child abuse scandal at Penn State University and the USA Gymnastics sex abuse scandal at Michigan State University; the discovery of academic fraud at the University of North Carolina at Chapel Hill; the alleged falsification of data by the Fox School of Business at Temple University in an effort to increase and maintain its national rankings in *U.S. News and World Report*; the student occupation of the administration building at Duke University; heightened racial tensions and campus unrest at the University of Missouri and Yale University; a cyberattack on the computer network at Rutgers University; allegations of widespread abuse by athletic coaches at the University of Maryland and the death of freshman offensive lineman Jordan McNair due to heatstroke suffered during a football workout; racist behavior within the Greek systems at the University of Oklahoma and Syracuse University and toward visiting high school students at Texas A&M University; evidence of Harvard University's men's soccer team ranking freshmen women by their appearance; allegations of widespread sexual assault at the University of Montana; and the investigation of eighty-five colleges and universities by the U.S. Department of Education for possible violations of Title IX (a federal antidiscrimination law protecting such victims). In addition to these specific incidents, multiple natural disasters and acts of campus violence have impacted colleges and universities across the country. This list merely scratches the surface of the types of incidents that have become crises of significance in recent years that are most relevant to colleges and universities, as will be discussed in the pages ahead.

In response to the frequency and complexity of crisis situations on college and university campuses, the American

Council on Education (ACE) convened a roundtable in 2012 with presidential leaders, media experts, and attorneys on the topic "Leading in Times of Crises." The results of this meeting led to an article (Bataille, Billings, & Nellum, 2012) and a subsequent book (Bataille & Cordova, 2014) on the subject. This topic remains a top priority for college and university leaders for many reasons. First, events or situations that are characterized as crises tend to have a dramatic impact on a wide array of organizational stakeholders. Next, these situations often influence the operations or finances of an organization, in addition to threatening the reputation of the institution. For example, based on recent research by Luca, Rooney, and Smith (2016), high-profile campus scandals led to approximately a 10 percent decline in student applications the following year. Two years after the high-profile racial protests at the University of Missouri, enrollment declined more than 35 percent, and budget cuts have forced the temporary closure of seven residence halls and the elimination of 400 staff positions (Hartocollis, 2017). A report on the sexual molestation case at Penn State indicated that the university and its insurers have spent $250 million—and counting—on fees related to the crisis, with $5.3 million spent on crisis communications and outside consultants alone (Mondics, 2017). Or consider the staggering $500 million settlement by Michigan State to the 332 survivors of sexual abuse committed by longtime university physician Larry Nassar (Smith & Hartocollis, 2018). In addition to the impact that crises have on stakeholders and the operations, finances, and reputation of the institution, crises have the potential to divert focus from the core educational mission of a college or university, as addressing them demands a great deal of time and energy from the leaders of the organization. As acknowledged by Rollo and Zdziarski (2007), "The impact of crises on the facilities and the institutions' ability to accomplish their educational mission must be addressed, but it is the human side of the equation that begs our attention as educators committed to serving our communities" (p. 3). These multifaceted consequences make organizational crises relevant moments for learning and development as leaders in higher education respond to, navigate, and learn from these events.

Crisis leadership in higher education is the subject of recent documentaries, such as *The Hunting Ground* (Ziering & Dick, 2015), and dissertations (Agnew, 2014; Garcia, 2015; Gill, 2012; Jacobsen, 2010; Menghini, 2014; Muffet-Willett, 2010). Despite the prevalence of crisis situations within the context of American colleges and universities, the scholarly literature in this area remains scarce, and the response to organizational crises is often the subject of widespread criticism. As suggested by Genshaft (2014), "higher education is particularly primed for poor handling of crises," in part due to lack of preparation, a decentralized governance structure, and an ongoing preoccupation with excellence that can prevent institutions from taking responsibility for these difficult situations (p. 10). This is consistent with the survey findings of Mitroff, Diamond, and Alpaslan (2006), which reveal a growing desire for improved understanding and practice as it relates to crisis leadership in higher education, particularly the need to identify and develop competencies and practices found to be most useful for effectively leading colleges and universities during these challenging and critical moments. The convergence of widespread public attention and inadequate preparation highlights the need for additional research in this area, one that this book may begin to fulfill.

Included in this volume is a research-informed crisis leadership framework that may be valuable for academic and administrative leaders in navigating crises that are most germane to institutions of higher education, highlighting the need to understand the core values of an institution, the historical context, and the types of leadership behaviors that preceded the crisis itself. Additional findings that will be presented include a taxonomy of crisis types that are most applicable to colleges and universities, a continuum for thinking through communication during crisis situations in higher education, and a scorecard of skills, values, and competencies required for effective crisis leadership.

Exploring Crises in Higher Education

Four research questions serve as a guide for this work:

1. What events/situations are characterized as crises in higher education?
2. How do these events/situations become defined and labeled as crises?
3. What are the prominent characteristics of the discourse around crisis and crisis leadership in higher education?
4. What skills, values, and competencies are important for the work of crisis leaders in higher education?

Answering these questions is critical to advancing our knowledge of the dynamics of crisis and the ways in which they are handled by leaders in higher education. Furthermore, these questions lead us to disentangle terms and labels that are often used interchangeably, such as crisis prevention, crisis management, and crisis leadership, in a way that can more adequately prepare aspiring and current leaders for the multifaceted practice of preventing, managing, and leading throughout the multiple stages of a crisis.

Before exploring the dynamics of leadership made prominent in crisis situations, it is important to first gain a clear understanding of the specific types of events that are characterized as crises in higher education. I sought to identify these types of events through a content analysis of higher education news outlets, including the *Chronicle of Higher Education* and *Inside Higher Ed*, and a smaller sample of articles from the *New York Times* and the *Wall Street Journal*. This search was limited to news articles published from 2011 to 2015 that included the word "crisis" or "crises" within the text, resulting in 489 articles in the *Chronicle of Higher Education* and 494 articles in *Inside Higher Ed*. Given the lack of a controlled vocabulary and the broader scope of both the *New York Times* and the *Wall Street Journal*, I reviewed a much smaller sample of the most recent fifty articles from these outlets using Factiva (2018), a global news database that would allow for a systematic search of the terms "crisis" or "crises" within higher education. The content analysis did not include articles unrelated to the specific topic of crisis in higher education.[1]

The remaining research questions interrogate the practice of crisis leadership and the ways in which leaders identify, characterize, and describe crises of significance facing institutions of higher education. In order to answer these questions, the second phase of this study consisted of semistructured interviews with thirty-seven senior university leaders representing a diversity of units from Association of American Universities (AAU) member institutions, which were selected for four primary reasons. First, the sixty-two institutions admitted into the AAU are recognized as leading public and private research institutions—those where one might expect to find well-developed best practices in the areas of crisis leadership preparation, expertise, and training and development opportunities, all of which might have an impact on the preparation and effectiveness of the leaders at these institutions. The scope of research, teaching, clinical, and outreach activities, including athletics, at these institutions gives rise to a broad range of potential crisis situations. Furthermore, because of their status as leaders of higher education, these institutions attract a great deal of media attention when crises occur and are subject to a great deal of scrutiny by a wide array of internal and external stakeholders. Finally, AAU member institutions serve as models for higher education across the country—and in some instances, the world—and in many respects, their rich history of academic excellence positions the universities as exemplars for other colleges and universities with similar research ambitions.

Each of the institutions included in this work had recently experienced a situation or event that was characterized as a crisis in the content analysis. Summarized in greater detail in chapter 4, these crises involve the areas of academics, athletics, clinical, technology, campus facilities, finance/business, human resources, leadership/governance, natural disasters, public safety, racial/identity conflict, or student affairs. In many instances, I also selected institutions where it was possible to draw upon existing relationships with colleagues in order to gain access to senior leaders who would be willing to participate in a study of this potentially sensitive topic. Finally, geographically close institutions were selected with the goal of conducting as many interviews as possible in person.[2]

In order to qualify for participation, respondents had to meet one of the following criteria:

- Serve as the senior leader(s) and administrator(s) most directly involved with the crisis at the institutional level
- Serve as the senior communication representative(s) most responsible for the design and delivery of messages during all phases of the university crisis

- Serve as the key university leader(s) from departments most affected by a particular crisis or set of crises

A majority of the individuals contacted for this study agreed to participate. Those who opted not to participate did so for several different reasons. In most instances, scheduling conflicts prohibited their participation. Others noted that they would not be able to contribute meaningfully to a study on this subject. Within each institution, a snowball sample approach was used to solicit the names of additional senior leaders with knowledge of and experience with a specific crisis situation (Lindlof & Taylor, 2011; Miles, Huberman, & Saldaña, 2014). The pool of interviewees consisted of senior leaders representing a variety of positions, responsibilities, and titles across the following divisions: Office of the Chancellor/President, Institutional Diversity, Facilities Management, Academic Affairs, University Marketing and Communications, Athletics, Information Technology, Student Affairs, Business and Administration, University Relations, and Alumni Relations.

Both content analysis and semistructured interviews were used because of the advantages they offer for this kind of project. Both methods allowed for a comprehensive and in-depth exploration into the area of crisis leadership in higher education. Specifically, these methods made it possible to analyze media reports of the landscape of higher education in the United States and then to more closely solicit and examine the experiences and perceptions of senior leaders involved in navigating the complexities of crisis situations at their respective institutions. Despite these advantages, both methods have limitations, which will be addressed in more detail in the concluding chapter of this book.[3]

Crisis Management and Crisis Leadership: The Value of a Communication Perspective

A crisis is viewed as an event, series of events, or situation that presents reputational risk to the institution and requires immediate attention on behalf of its leaders. Crisis is also a socially constructed, often subjective, and communicative phenomenon. The framework to be developed here suggests that incidents happen and that crises are created through communication; consequently, it is through communication that they must be addressed. Crises are distinct from problems, nuisances, or incidents; yet, as will be discussed, the labeling of events as "crises," the monitoring of events that may escalate to the level of crisis, and the preparation of leaders for navigating the inherent ambiguity and mission-related significance associated with crisis situations in higher education are much less clear and potentially more problematic measures. The ubiquity of crisis in higher education, coupled with the subjectivity of the term itself, provides an opportunity to consider a broader view of crisis leadership—a perspective that foregrounds the many communicative elements of leadership in higher education in a way that involves, but extends beyond, reputation management.

Much of the scholarly literature in the areas of crisis management and crisis communication comes from the domain of public relations, as it is traditionally understood—how to protect the reputation of the institution, maintain a favorable impression in the eyes of many stakeholders, and use communication to shape public opinion. Unlike existing projects that characterize communication as a tool for managing specific components of crisis situations in their aftermath, this book places a broadened emphasis on the role of communication in the ongoing practice of crisis leadership. As described herein, the construct of crisis leadership includes—and builds upon—the reputation-oriented focus of crisis management in a way that more fully captures the process of anticipating, preventing, responding to, and learning from the seemingly endless stream of events that challenge the reputation, integrity, and values of a college or university, and its leaders, before, during, and after a crisis event. In short, the management of messages and the protection of reputations are necessary leadership functions, but they do not tell the full story of what is involved in leading during times of crisis.

In addition to exploring the meaning of crisis leadership in higher education, this text offers a reaction to the objective treatment of crisis as widely acknowledged and supported in the scholarly and professional literature. The framework introduced here presents crisis as a contested, subjective, and communicative phenomenon, with the goal of enriching our understanding of how the term "crisis" is used and to what end. Just as leadership emerges from the interplay of both leaders and followers, the very notion of crisis is subject to the same negotiation between higher education leaders and the many internal and external audiences who are most influenced by the crisis situation itself. This negotiation calls for research that untangles the choice to use the label "crisis" from the realities of the phenomenon being described. As a discursive framing strategy (Fairhurst, 2011a; Fairhurst & Sarr, 1996), affected stakeholders, the media, and organizational leaders may use the crisis label for any number of reasons. For those affected by an incident, for example, framing the event as a crisis helps to focus attention on a problem of concern and heighten the probability of an expedited response. For the media, framing an event as a crisis signals its significance and news value. From the perspective of the institution and its leaders, the declaration of a crisis can have advantages. For instance, leaders may find it strategically useful to identify a phenomenon as a crisis because of its ability to invoke leadership shortcuts, permit expedited decision making, and facilitate quick and authoritative action. For any or all of these reasons, crises may be proclaimed *and* problematized in higher education practice.

The questions addressed in this study are important to the literature in communication, leadership and organizational studies, and higher education. I approach the study of crisis leadership in higher education from an organizational communication perspective, whereby organizations and leadership are understood to be communicative accomplishments (Fairhurst, 2007; Fairhurst & Putnam, 2004), and the "organization is constituted by the interaction processes among its members" (Langley & Tsoukas, 2010, p. 4). As crisis and risk communication scholar Matt Seeger shares in the opening article in the new *Journal of International Crisis and Risk Communication Research*, a communication-centered understanding of crisis and risk is essential for two reasons: "First, communication is necessary for meaning making around what are very uncertain and equivocal events. Second, communication is instrumental as part of the crisis and risk management functions" (Seeger, 2018, p. 7). Thus, based on this line of thinking, communication serves as both a conceptual orientation into how crises are understood and a specific function through which crises are managed. Much of the recent scholarship on the topic of crisis communication within higher education can be found in the public relations (Fortunato, 2008; Leeper & Leeper, 2006; Len-Rios, 2010) and higher education literatures (Coombs, 2008; Dubois, 2006; Garcia, 2015; Gill, 2012; Jablonski, McClellan, & Zdziarski, 2008; Mann, 2007; Muffet-Willett, 2010; Zdziarski, Dunkel, & Rollo 2007). My treatment of this topic attempts to highlight both elements of communication that are manifested in crisis leadership—the meaning making, interpretation, and social construction of the crisis event, and the process through which leadership is made possible. From this unique vantage point, I hope to provide a richer understanding of the processes by which crises emerge and to clarify the contexts within which leadership and organization occur across institutions of higher education.

Overview of the Book

This book was written with several audiences in mind. First, for individuals interested in understanding the dynamics of crisis and leadership in higher education, it provides a bridge between theoretical concepts and practical insights in a way that can help to advance scholarship and professional practice in this area. Second, for leadership educators with an interest in the subject, the concepts, models, and research findings highlighted herein can be used to organize crisis leadership development programs and initiatives that are theory-informed and that align with contemporary issues of interest. Finally, for any current or aspiring leaders who may be facing or may one day encounter crisis situations, it is my hope that the insights offered in this book will be of use to the many individuals who fulfill these challenging and critically important leadership roles across institutions of higher education.

Looking ahead, chapter 2, "The Social Construction of Crisis in Higher Education: The Perception of Crisis, the Reality of Crisis," explores the subject of crisis as a social construction. The "crisis" label is typically used to describe an existing external phenomenon, event, or situation; however, as detailed in this chapter, the lens of social construction allows for a consideration of the ways in which leaders recognize an event or a series of events as constituting a crisis. Crises exist because of the ways in which people perceive a situation or because of the ways that leaders talk about certain event(s). Thus, the idea of social construction shifts from a view of crises being external phenomena that are imposed on an organization to a way of thinking that recognizes that all crises are constituted through communication between leaders and followers. This theoretical framework will provide a context for the remainder of the book.

In order to explore the various definitions of crisis and the process by which these crises are identified and described, I asked senior administrators these two questions: (1) What does the word "crisis" mean to you, thinking particularly about the context of higher education? (2) What factors/conditions play a role in treating a particular event or set of events as a crisis to which leaders must pay particular attention and respond? The emergent themes from the interview data are summarized in chapter 3, "The Process of Defining and Labeling Phenomena as Crises," which addresses the multiple and often conflicting definitions of crises and the ways that senior leaders in higher education differentiate crises from incidents, nuisances, or problems based on their severity.

Myriad incidents or situations are typically classified as crises in higher education—crises that are crosscutting in nature—based on the taxonomy enumerated earlier: academics, athletics, clinical, technological, facilities, financial/business, human resources, leadership/governance, natural disasters, public safety, racial/identity conflict, and student affairs. Chapter 4, "The Characterization and Categorization of Crises in Higher Education," describes this schema in greater detail, drawing on both media descriptions of the crisis situations and relevant interview data to support this taxonomy.

As noted, this book is anchored in communication theories, concepts, and principles. Chapter 5, "Centrality of Communication in the Theory and Practice of Crisis Leadership," explores the major communicative findings to emerge from this study. These findings, coupled with the growing body of scholarship on leadership communication, crisis communication, and crisis leadership, led to the development of the Crisis Leadership Communication Continuum described in the chapter. The continuum illustrates the range in crisis communication behaviors from compliance to dialogue, with self-focus and other-focus positioned on opposite ends of the continuum. The model is meant to illustrate two opposing tensions that leaders must negotiate when communicating with internal and external audiences during all phases of a perceived crisis situation.

The notion of crisis leadership, particularly crisis leadership in higher education, extends beyond reputation management, crisis prevention, and the public relations–oriented management of a unit, department, or institutional crisis, as supported by the diverse and broad array of required competencies, skills, and values described in chapter 6, "Crisis Adaptation of Leadership Competencies Scorecard for Leaders in Higher Education." The tendency to privilege reputational implications over the many other requisite crisis leadership behaviors is not only limiting, but may also be detrimental to an individual's overall leadership effectiveness. As one senior administrator suggested, this tendency is problematic because it leads administrators to consider "not what is the right thing to do, but what impact is this going to have." This chapter highlights the broad portfolio of competencies required for leadership during these critical, public, and high-stakes moments of organizational disruption.

And finally, chapter 7, "Implications for Effective Crisis Leadership in Higher Education," summarizes the concepts, principles, and takeaways from this study that have implications for the practice of crisis leadership in higher education. Several of these implications include the need for

- a more serious consideration of stakeholder perceptions
- the adoption of an institutional scope
- high-performing incident response teams
- agility in higher education leadership, which at times may seem countercultural
- an infrastructure for using and monitoring social media activity
- intentional learning based on crises and crisis leadership across organizational sectors

The book concludes with a message of hope, for, despite the many complications and challenges that exist, American colleges and universities remain widely regarded as among the finest in the world. To a certain extent, these institutions are also held to a higher standard than other types of organizations. Crises shift the national, and at times international, spotlight to these institutions. These critical moments of organizational disruption provide an opportunity for leaders to model and reaffirm the values and principles that are most consistent with the mission of higher education. To succeed in this effort, it will be increasingly important for communication, higher education, and leadership scholars and practitioners to more seriously consider the complexity and nuance of crisis and crisis leadership in higher education and their implications for effective crisis leadership practice.

Conclusion

Crisis communication remains a primary area of study within the public relations literature for obvious reasons; however, there is an important element to crisis leadership that deserves our attention. Crises provide a rich backdrop within which to explore the interdependent relationship among colleges and universities, the distributed nature of leadership in higher education, and an increasingly complex and generally unpredictable environment. In short, the study of crisis in higher education offers a germane, compelling, and multifaceted context for leadership analysis.

As mentioned by one senior administrator who was interviewed for this project, "The whole lived experience of the human condition exists on our college campuses 24/7. In an era when we practice our work to be all in support of our communities, I think that means that we have to be prepared to be crisis-driven." This book comes at a critical time for American higher education—one that is marked by significant change across the sector, ongoing scrutiny from a wide array of internal and external stakeholders, and much public debate regarding race relations, freedom of speech, and issues of access, affordability, and accountability across colleges and universities. Heeding this interviewee's call to become "crisis-driven," this book seeks to contribute to a richer understanding of what fundamentally constitutes crisis in higher education, along with a more nuanced understanding of the primary issues at stake for leaders during these critical moments.

In their summary of the six challenges facing organizational communication scholarship, Jones, Watson, Gardner, and Gallois (2004) called for increased scholarship that "must be useful to people in ongoing organizations," notably research that considers the increasingly important role of context (p. 725). This sentiment is shared by others who call for communication research to be consequential (Daly, 2000), to "reflect far more stridently on the relevance of practice" (Zelizer, 2015, p. 414), and to be praxis-based and praxis-oriented as a practical discipline that "cultivates critical, creative, and well-informed deliberation on normative and technical aspects of practical conduct" (Craig, 2018, p. 289). Communication scholarship can have a lasting impact by spanning practice and theory; thus, this book aspires to be "consequential" for higher education leadership theory and practice. The study of the discourse surrounding crisis situations in higher education, and the subsequent leadership values, competencies, and behaviors that are found to be most critical to navigating these types of situations, can contribute to the growing body of scholarship, training and development initiatives, and best practices in this area.

Reflection Questions for Consideration

1. Why is the study of this topic one of personal, professional, and/or intellectual interest? What do you hope to learn, and in what ways do you hope to enhance your own leadership skills by reading this text? At the end of each chapter, revisit your response to these questions as a way of tracking your progress on these learning and/or practice goals.
2. What institutional or environmental factors do you believe are contributing to the increase in the magnitude, frequency, and complexity of crises (Helsloot et al., 2012)?
3. Identify a crisis of significance an institution of higher education is currently facing. Based on your current knowledge of crisis management and crisis leadership, how would you evaluate the effectiveness of the response to the crisis? What factors contribute to your assessment of the effectiveness or ineffectiveness of the leader's response to the event or situation?

2

The Social Construction of Crisis in Higher Education

The Perception of Crisis, the Reality of Crisis

Crises are unpredictable phenomena, yet not unexpected (Coombs, 2015). Within the world of higher education, we have come to anticipate the occurrence of crisis situations, and despite our best efforts, situations perceived to be crises continue to occur across our institutions. In most cases, protocols and plans are in place to help guide the response to situations involving such occurrences as active shooters, natural disasters, and disorderly campus protests. At the same time, planning and preparation processes continue to evolve based on trends in the broader environment—consider how colleges and universities have adopted sophisticated communication alert systems in the aftermath of the 2007 shootings at Virginia Tech, or the development of new child protection policies and reporting procedures in response to the 2012 child sex abuse scandal at Penn State. Although there is general agreement that crises are problematic and potentially disruptive, there is a lack of consensus when it comes to defining a crisis. In many ways, everyone's perspective of crisis is influenced by each individual's professional role and responsibilities, personal history with crisis-like situations, and the tolerance that he or she has developed to best deal with the conditions that arise.

I have come to consider the ways in which an understanding of crisis as a social construction can be useful in better understanding the fluid and dynamic nature of these types of occurrences. An argument can be made that crises exist because of the ways in which people perceive an event or situation or because of the ways that leaders talk about it, and the adoption of a social construction lens encourages a shift in how we understand crisis, distinguishing external phenomena that are "out there" from those that are constituted through communication between leaders and followers and between the media and internal/external stakeholders. From this perspective, the language of social construction allows us to consider the many perceptions of crisis, the various ways in which leaders recognize one event or a series of events as crises, and the potential strategies for addressing crises that best meet the needs of these broadly interpreted occasions of complexity. In this chapter I provide a preview of the etymology of the word "crisis," a summary of existing research on the various ways in which crisis situations unfold, and an overview of the central social construction principles that will help set the stage for the remainder of the book.

The Evolution of "Crisis"

The etymology of the word "crisis" reflects the evolution of our understanding of the phenomenon and the shifting emotional perceptions toward crisis situations. The word "crisis" has its roots in the Greek language, where it represents a "turning point," similar to the medical usage of the term in

Latin to imply the turning point of an illness. Unlike the negative connotation currently associated with crises, the word originally referred to the optimistic turning point in times of sickness, tragedy, or peril. As a result of the contributions of human choices, decisions, or behaviors, these turning points could meaningfully contribute to the future of an individual or organization (Shrivastava, 1993). Beginning in the eighteenth century, the word "crisis" evolved to signify a difficult situation or dilemma—a "turning point" oriented toward decline and destruction, rather than one of hope or opportunity. Ulmer, Sellnow, and Seeger (2018) emphasize the role of crises as "unique moments in the history of organizations" (p. 5) that are distinguished from other unpleasant circumstances because of three factors: surprise, threat, and short response time (Hermann, 1963). Borrowing from the Chinese interpretation of crisis, "wei chi" translates to "dangerous opportunity" (Sellnow & Seeger, 2013), and we can see how these "unique moments" are cloaked in fear, danger, and uncertainty as individuals and organizations approach these defining turning points. Crises—and manifestations of conflict more generally—serve as communicative moments of "awakening" that have the potential to "make us alert" (Arnett, Bell McManus, & McKendree, 2013). This ongoing tension between danger and opportunity gave rise to the development of the field of crisis management—where the primary goals include both minimizing danger and maximizing opportunity.

The causes associated with any crisis are complex and multifaceted, leading Seeger, Sellnow, and Ulmer (2003) to categorize three primary ones: (1) normal failure and interactive complexity; (2) failures in foresight, warnings, and risk perception; and (3) breakdowns in vigilance. Seymour and Moore (2000) identify two distinct types of crisis: "the cobra," a sudden crisis that takes an organization by surprise, and "the python," a slowly creeping crisis that grows increasingly problematic over time (p. 10). Regardless of the cause, the perception of the increase in organizational crises parallels Perrow's (1984) prediction that the increased complexity in society would also lead to an increase in accidents and crises. Just as organizations become increasingly complex, so too do the environments in which these organizations are situated. These increasingly contentious ecosystems, marked by a 24/7 news cycle, immediate access to information, and the use of various new technologies, are seemingly ripe for the emergence of occurrences that many may perceive to be crisis-like in nature.

In her writing on the prevalence of crisis situations in our contemporary environment and the stakes involved by identifying these occurrences as crises, Roitman (2014) describes crisis as "an omnipresent sign in almost all forms of narrative today [that] is mobilized as the defining category of historical situations, past and present" (p. 3). Invoking crisis as an object of knowledge enables and forecloses certain narratives and communicative possibilities. As Roitman posits, "Under the sign of crisis, 'events' are distinguished and signified; they achieve empirical status as 'history' and hence become legible to us" (p. 93). The identification of a particular incident or moment as a crisis involves a level of judgment, leading it to become a widely used—and potentially overused—label (Gigliotti & Fortunato, 2017). Thus, as we consider the ways in which our understanding of crisis evolved—from an optimistic and forward-looking turning point to one marked by fear, danger, and paralysis—we must pause and carefully consider what is at stake in our analysis of contemporary events or situations as potential crises facing higher education.

Stages of a Crisis

In order to better understand the socially constructed nature of crises, it is worth exploring how scholars have characterized the various stages within which these events unfold. An understanding of the crisis life cycle can inform how crises are interpreted as such at various points in a sequence. Borrowing from the work on chaos theory, there exist an underlying order and pattern within the disorder of crisis (Li & Yorke, 1975; Lorenz, 1963; Wheatley, 2006). This order and pattern often become coherent only in the aftermath of crisis situations, as individuals engage in processes of enactment where situations and moments become bracketed and where retrospective sensemaking of these previous situations occurs (Weick, 1988). The sensemaking literature allows us to think through how crises are escalated and de-escalated based on the ways in which one constructs what then is made sensible, memorable, or an object of our attention. As Weick goes on to note, "To sort out a crisis as it unfolds often requires action which simultaneously generates the raw material that is used for sensemaking and affects the unfolding crisis itself" (p. 305).

In a widely publicized example, African American student activists and allies confronted then University of Missouri system president Timothy M. Wolfe at a homecoming parade on October 10, 2015, demanding that he acknowledge the plight of minority students following a host of racially motivated incidents on the campus. Wolfe's failure to exit the car and directly address these student concerns—concerns that have a much deeper, historical, and long-standing significance (Fortunato, Gigliotti, & Ruben, 2018)—sparked a cascading set of protests and calls for his resignation. His response reflects an act of retrospective sensemaking, which unfortunately came nearly a month after the homecoming incident: "I regret my reaction at the MU homecoming parade when the Concerned Student 1950 group approached my car. I am sorry, and my apology is long overdue. My behavior seemed like I did not care. That was not my intention. I was caught off guard in that moment. Nonetheless, had I gotten out of the car to acknowledge the students and talk with them perhaps we wouldn't be where we are today" (Deere & Addo, 2015). Following the boycott of university dining and retail services by students in the Concerned Student 1950 group (named for the first year that African Americans were admitted to Missouri), a hunger strike led by graduate student Jonathan Butler, and the boycott of the university football team (Deere & Addo, 2015), both the university president and the chancellor resigned. This example is one of many that highlight the significance of sensemaking processes throughout the evolution of crisis situations. In looking back, the unwieldy and unpredictable moments of the past become more coherent, more orderly.

A crisis has the potential to unfold in any number of ways and across any number of punctuated phases—and based on one's interpretation of the crisis event or string of events, these phases influence how one thinks about crisis and the actions one may or may not take in response to it. For example, Fink (1986) uses the progression of a medical illness to depict the four common stages of a crisis:

- prodromal—clues or hints of a potential crisis begin to emerge;
- crisis breakout or acute—a triggering event occurs along with the attendant damage;
- chronic—the effects of the crisis linger as efforts to handle it progress;

- resolution—the conclusion of the crisis, with some clear signal that the crisis is no longer a concern to stakeholders.

A second model, introduced by Mitroff (1994), divides crisis management into five distinct phases:

- signal detection
- probing and prevention
- damage containment
- recovery
- learning

With the exception of the added emphasis on learning as a separate phase, Mitroff's proposed crisis cycle mirrors Fink's findings. Finally, Coombs (2015) identifies a third way of thinking about the evolution of crisis:

- pre-crisis
- crisis event
- post-crisis

Each of the three phases is instructive. Together, they provide a coherent ordering of crisis moments; yet, crises, by their very nature, are unpredictable and call for leaders to be both flexible and prepared (Gigliotti & Fortunato, 2017). There is a propensity, supported by these various models, to depict crisis as a linear process, and by doing so, a series of prescriptive strategies for managing crisis situations emerges based on one's placement in this cycle (Gigliotti, 2016). The following higher education example illustrates some of the challenges presented when crisis is interpreted as a linear process with a demarcated and identifiable beginning and end:

In the child abuse sex scandal at Penn State, the public announcement of the many allegations against the former assistant football coach might be viewed as the commencement of the crisis. However, as outlined in the Freeh Report commissioned by the Penn State Board of Trustees, critical facts relating to Coach Jerry Sandusky's child abuse were concealed from and by leaders across the university—a troubling finding that points to the many historical factors leading to the public components of the crisis. . . . This case is one of many that capture the subjectivity involved in defining something as a *crisis*, let alone identifying its beginning and end. (Gigliotti & Fortunato, 2017, pp. 305-306)

Or, referring to the earlier example from the University of Missouri, it is difficult to determine and isolate when the crisis began. Some might see the actions (or lack thereof) by President Wolfe in response to the homecoming protest as the start of the crisis, whereas others may point to the student boycotts, hunger strike, or actions by the football teams as the origin of the crisis. The language of social construction helps to move beyond prescriptive and formulaic approaches to crisis management based on one's phase in a crisis life cycle toward a more emergent and individualized understanding of crisis where both leadership and communication are made more prominent, and where the broadened focus extends to an exploration of the historical conditions that led to the invocation of crisis—conditions that may not be as clearly presented in the above-mentioned life cycles. For both the Penn State and University of Missouri cases, a history preceded both high-profile incidents, including what some have characterized as a culture of secrecy at Penn State (Pérez-Peña, 2011) and a culture of racial tension at Mizzou (Marans & Stewart, 2015), and a more complete understanding of crisis leadership must take account of these antecedent conditions.

Deconstructing Symbolic Interaction and the Social Construction of Reality

In their introduction to the chapter on leadership communication in the updated *SAGE Handbook of Organizational Communication*, Fairhurst and Connaughton (2014b) acknowledge a new complexity associated with the study of leadership—a complexity that is marked by focusing not solely on the individual leader but on all organizational actors involved in leadership exchanges and experiences. Efforts to address what were considered inherent limitations of the positivist research tradition led to increased thinking and writing on the nature of language in constituting one's reality, what has been referred to as the "linguistic turn" in the social and organizational sciences. One result of this pivot in philosophical thought was an added emphasis on the relationship between philosophy and language (Alvesson & Kärreman, 2000; Rorty, 1967). The emphasis shifted from an understanding of the physical properties of an object or phenomenon toward the language used to speak about the object or phenomenon (Ayer, 1936; Wittgenstein, 1961). As noted by Fairhurst (2009), "Those impacted by the linguistic turn are broadly social constructionist, discursive, and more qualitative than mainstream leadership scholars" (p. 1608). These approaches to leadership tend to position communication as being constitutive of leadership itself (Fairhurst and Connaughton, 2014b, p. 406). From this point of view, communication is both a tool used by leaders and an orientation through which leadership is made possible, with followers playing a critical role in the ongoing construction of leadership processes. In addition, as it relates to the social construction of crisis, this line of thinking can be extended further to consider the leadership function of the media in shaping the perception of reality for direct and indirect audiences.

Social interaction is a natural condition of the human experience. Similar to Thayer's (1968) definition of communication, human actors who interact with one another must also take into account what the other is thinking, expecting, and doing—what Blumer (2003) describes as "a process of ongoing activity in which participants are developing lines of action in the multitudinous situations they encounter" (p. 151). The position of symbolic interactionism is that the meaning of the things toward which people act is critical and worthy of analysis and exploration. Symbolic interaction, according to Blumer, contains three central premises, including the following: "The first premise is that human beings act toward things on the basis of the meanings that the things have for them. . . . The second premise is that the meaning of such things is derived from, or arises out of, the social interaction that one has with one's fellows. The third premise is that these meanings are handled in, and modified through, an interpretative process used by the person in dealing with the things he [or she] encounters" (p. 135).

Reality is thus not seen as a given, but rather consists of acts of interpretation, definition, and action/reaction (Blumer, 1966; Mead, 1934). The communication and leadership implications of this theory are significant, particularly in light of this current exploration into the dynamics of crisis leadership in higher education. As supported by Arnett et al. (2013), "In the praxis of leadership, one cannot ignore either theoretical or practical examples of meaning in action" (p. 34). Symbolic interactionism creates a prism through which one can consider the ways that human actors—or leaders more specifically—respond to situations and stakeholders based on the meaning that these situations or stakeholders have for them. Interpretation leads one to act in a particular way, and, as detailed in the following paragraphs, the impact of followers in the ongoing process of leadership should not be ignored or underestimated.

With roots in both symbolic interactionism (Mead, 1934) and phenomenology (Schutz, 1970), a social construction lens highlights how people make their social and cultural worlds just as these worlds make them, and language takes on a constitutive role in this social process (Berger & Luckmann, 1966; Gergen, 1999; Hacking, 1999; Potter, 1996; Shotter, 1993). In their synthesis of the literature, Fairhurst and Grant (2010) describe how "communication becomes more than a simple transmission; it is a medium by which the negotiation and construction of meaning takes place" (p. 174). According to Grint (2005), contingency theories of leadership that isolate the leader, context, situation, and followers are inherently limited, and he calls for more attention to be paid to "the role of leaders and decision-makers in the construction of contexts that legitimates their intended or executed actions and accounts" (p. 1472). This is an especially important observation as we consider the nature of crisis. There is a tendency to use the label "crisis" in our descriptions of existing external phenomena, events, or situations—the natural disaster that devastated the college campus or the active shooter who triggered alarm across the institution, for example; however, the lens of social construction, as previously described, allows for consideration of the ways in which leaders *and* followers recognize an event or series of events as constituting crisis. More specifically, crises exist because of the ways in which formal and informal leaders and the media talk about the situation and the ways in which internal and external audiences perceive the situation. Thus, the idea of social construction shifts the focus of crisis from phenomena that are "out there" to those that are constituted through communication between leaders and followers and between the media and internal/external stakeholders. This perspective recognizes those crises that intensely and publicly disrupt the normal operations of an institution, such as natural disasters or active shooters, while also taking into consideration the more emergent types of crises that also require the immediate attention of leaders, such as viral social media campaigns, incidents of racial unrest, or allegations of sexual assault.

One final point deserves mention here. Leadership is not limited to those at the top of the organizational hierarchy; rather, as a process of social influence, leadership may be accomplished by any organizational actor, shaped by verbal and nonverbal communication, and co-constructed between leaders and followers (Ruben & Gigliotti, 2016). Leadership activity is distributed throughout the organization, as is typical for institutions of higher education, and it is arguably socially constructed through communication within the organization. This understanding of leadership aligns with the definition presented by Barge and Fairhurst (2008), who define leadership as "a co-created, performative, contextual, and attributional process where the ideas articulated in talk or action are recognized by others as progressing tasks that are important to them" (p. 232). A relational conceptualization of leadership suggests that leadership is generated through interactions among people—variously labeled leader and follower—in a particular context (Fairhurst, 2007; Fairhurst & Uhl-Bien, 2012). A myriad of examples from within the context of higher education speak to the importance of how major decisions are often negotiated in a way that reflects both a leader's interpretation of a situation *and* the role of the followers in shaping the outcome of the decision. One might consider the removal—and eventual reinstatement—of President Teresa Sullivan at the University of Virginia for criticism related to her rate of institutional adaptation and change. Another example includes the appointment—and eventual withdrawal—of Dr. Steven Salaita at the University of Illinois at Urbana-Champaign because of the tone of his comments on Twitter about Israel's policies in Gaza. These examples represent the complex, uncertain, and messy nature of decision making in higher education—a context that is known for its multiple missions and diverse array of stakeholders with conflicting needs and expectations (Birnbaum, 1988, 1992; Gmelch, 2013; Gmelch & Buller, 2015; Gmelch & Miskin, 2004; Lawrence, 2006; Manning, 2012; Ruben, 2004). The outcome of these decisions extends beyond a leader's interpretation of a situation and involves the role of the followers in helping to co-construct the environments within which leaders operate. The concepts of symbolic interactionism and social constructionism underscore the importance of communicative practices, broaden the context for leadership theory and practice to consider the formative role of the follower(s), and provide various conceptual tools for the analysis of leadership communication throughout all phases of a given crisis.

The Social Construction of Crisis

This summary of key findings from my research further illustrates the intersections between the theory of social construction and the dynamics of crisis in higher education. Senior leaders who participated in this project were asked the following questions:

1. What reactions from internal and external stakeholders may elevate an issue or event to the level of crisis?

2. Do you think that the way in which leaders talk about events can make them seem more like or less like a crisis? Why or why not?

3. When communicating to internal or external audiences during an ongoing problematic event, would you resist using the term "crisis"? Why or why not? When would it be appropriate to adopt that term? What are the implications of calling an ongoing problem/set of problems a "crisis"? Are there disadvantages to labeling something as a crisis?

The responses to these questions are organized around three themes related to (a) the perception of crisis, (b) the ways in which leaders and the media frame crisis situations, and (c) the role of crisis as a self-fulfilling prophecy. As characterized by many of the respondent comments, the invocation of crisis has the potential to heighten emotions, attract attention, and create the conditions through which one experiences crisis-like situations. For these reasons, as detailed below, a communication-oriented exploration into the social construction of crisis considers the ways in which leaders and those who report on crisis situations talk about these critical moments for an organization and its stakeholders.

THE PERCEPTION OF CRISIS, THE REALITY OF CRISIS

As noted, crises are said to exist because of the ways in which various audiences perceive the situation and because of the ways that formal and informal leaders talk about the situation. As one senior administrator posited: "When you're in the middle of it, you need to pay attention to it. Time is of the essence. Crisis is only flamed by a lack of immediate attention. Recognizing it as a crisis is part of that. I think the time starts to tick away. You have to trust that even if you're the leader, if someone else sees something as a crisis, you have to listen" (Participant 23).[1] This claim was reinforced by another administrator from University Relations, who suggested the following:

> Know what it is that you're dealing with and then consult others. By God, we're not the smartest people in the world, and get that team around you who will see it differently than you do because if the crisis is me or I'm so into it, I might just not be able to see clearly what I could do or how people are reacting because I'm defensive about it or I'm emotionally involved in it. Don't under-react, don't overreact. Get the facts, get the right team around you, and do it in a hurry. You can't wait on this crap because it's going to move faster than you. (Participant 27)

The data illustrate how the perception of crisis contributes to the existence of crisis, and as indicated by numerous interview participants in this project, the crisis—as a socially constructed and communicative phenomenon—takes on a life of its own as leaders attend—or fail to attend—to the situation at hand.

A related idea to emerge from the data suggests that it is a leadership imperative to treat phenomena that others perceive to be crises with attention, scrutiny, and a general degree of seriousness. For example, senior leaders addressed this process accordingly: "The perception often makes the reality" (Participant 1); "When [a situation] gets elevated because it's part of the public discourse in the news media, that becomes a crisis that we have to deal with" (Participant 12); and "If others perceive something to be a crisis, it is a crisis" (Participant 3). This sentiment helps to explain the inadequate response by the president of the University of Missouri, who failed to adequately acknowledge the very serious perspectives of the student protesters during the homecoming parade. Perceptions of crisis matter, and as the Missouri case and many others illustrate, the failure to recognize these perceptions can aggravate an already serious situation.

The ingredients and conditions for crisis exist across colleges and universities, and part of the challenge involves the ability to gauge stakeholder perceptions in the midst of troubling circumstances. As one administrator described in an interview, "That's the world we live in now. It's tough. You really don't know what's a crisis that's unfolding before you" (Participant 4). Although crisis was broadly interpreted and defined, there was general agreement among the administrators that "crisis is in the eye of the beholder" (Participant 36), and given this subjective dimension, "it behooves us to have institutional leaders in agreement about what constitutes a crisis. I need to have my finger on the pulse of a president, and my colleague vice presidents, to have us all understand what we are going to deem a crisis" (Participant 21).

THE FRAMING OF CRISIS BY LEADERS AND THE MEDIA

As Weick (1995) and others have suggested, leaders (and the media at large) often create the realities to which they must then respond, and for Fairhurst (2011b), a meaning-centered rather than transmission-centered understanding of communication allows us to "embrace the skill of framing as the way in which we fashion [the co-creation of] meaning to create realities to which we must then respond" (p. 47). A second theme to emerge from the data relates to the impact of framing a situation or event as a crisis. Fairhurst describes this act of framing as the "ability to shape the meaning of a subject—typically, the situation here and now—to judge its character and significance through the meanings chosen," which in turn shapes reality for those involved in this co-constructed process. When asked to describe their use of the "crisis" label, one person noted, "In probably nine cases out of ten, we make things into crises" (Participant 1). Many administrators indicated that the decision to call something a crisis is often intentional and deliberate. One senior finance and business leader suggested the following:

> I don't avoid [using the "crisis" label]. I try to be parsimonious about it. I mean, it's a term that I would, again, reserve only for those things that come upon you that are deserving of that label by nature of their impact and their ability to sort of garner notoriety. It's not something that you affix lightly to something that presents itself. There are also times when something deserves that label. Sometimes there needs to be truth in labeling so that you get people's attention. For instance, if I go to [the president], and I say, "This issue has the potential to become a full-blown crisis if this isn't addressed quickly," I want his antenna to go up because my use of that term is intentional. (Participant 10)

As another vice president noted, "We have to define it as what the consequences or unintended consequences are to call it a crisis. I think a crisis is also a terrible thing to waste" (Participant 23). As we recall the etymological roots of "crisis," the interview data suggest that opportunity exists within crisis—and one might extend this further based on the data to suggest that opportunity exists within the framing of crisis.

Leaders in higher education and media professionals who are responsible for writing and reporting on these critical incidents must recognize the responsibility of their framing decisions. The interview data captured the many emotions that accompany crisis-like phenomena, and as reinforced by several administrators, the decision to characterize an event or situation as a crisis contributes to these emotions. As one Academic Affairs administrator described this leadership responsibility: "How a leader comes across is extremely important, especially early when the events unfold, because nobody really knows what the truth is at that time. It's very difficult. Everybody's in a panic. The leader's job is to control as much fear, and make sure people are safe. So yes, the leader is critically important. People know about things well before the facts are known. You can easily create a crisis situation when it's not really a crisis situation" (Participant 4). This sentiment was shared by a chief information officer, who noted the following: "I do think that sometimes situations are labeled crises, but you have to take the time to sort of level set and make sure they are. Because sometimes they are, and sometimes they're not" (Participant 8). This framing decision often carries significant responsibility for its ability to shape both the perception and the reality associated with the circumstances at hand. The findings from this project point to the importance of considering not just the crisis-like situation facing colleges and universities and their leaders, but also the ways in which the event is situated (Grint, 2005).

One additional idea related to this theme deserves mention. The framing of an event or situation as a crisis by a leader is often reserved for the most serious of situations. One vice president for Student Affairs indicated that this decision may not necessarily be a conscious or intentional one, but that "we don't use [the word "crisis"] a lot. . . . I have heard a lot of words like 'tragedy,' but not 'crisis.' We, in our incident response planning, we use [the word 'tragedy'] more than we talk about 'crisis response planning.' I don't think we shy away from the word, I just don't know that we tend to use it all of the time" (Participant 14). As discussed in more detail in the next chapter, there was general agreement among the respondents that crises threaten reputations, impact the lives of those involved in the institution, and disrupt the ways in which the organization functions. To this point, there is an element of risk involved in the communication around crisis-like phenomena, such as the following risk described by another senior Student Affairs leader: "In one direction it could be to inflame something that really didn't need to be inflamed because of the rhetoric around that, but the other could be to downplay it and create a backlash around the downplaying that creates its own crisis. The communication is critical, and it can work against you in either direction" (Participant 35). This seems to suggest an idea described in more detail in the following section, that the communicative choice to frame some event or situation as a crisis carries consequences. These findings speak to the leader's ability— and ethical responsibility—to "manage meaning" during crisis-like situations (Fairhurst, 2007, 2011a; Fairhurst & Sarr, 1996; Smircich & Morgan, 1982).

CRISIS AS A SELF-FULFILLING PROPHECY

The idea of crisis as a self-fulfilling prophecy is the third noteworthy theme related to the communicative construction of crisis, in that the communication surrounding crisis heightens emotions, attracts attention, and creates the conditions through which one experiences crisis-like situations. Several claims made in the interviews addressed the connotations associated with the word "crisis" and the internal and external impacts of using this label to describe the state of affairs in higher education. According to the interview data, there is something inherently provocative associated with the use of the "crisis" label, and the decision to call something a crisis can intentionally or unintentionally trigger public attention. As described by a chief of staff to the chancellor, "Crisis sells papers. Crisis is a word that I think resonates with the public and makes you want to read it. Provocative in such a way, like 'oh my God,' higher ed is in a serious situation" (Participant 3). The desire or tendency for the media to sensationalize crisis emerged as a prevalent theme in this project. According to one leader from Student Affairs, "The news trucks show up. 'Oh my gosh, it's a crisis.' The news trucks showing up does not mean that there really is a crisis. What they're looking for, and they love to come out here and do man on the street interviews to see if they can get a student to say, 'oh it's horrible.' Then sometimes we have a tendency to react to that" (Participant 13). Another individual pointed out that higher education news outlets are "like every news media outlet. They have an incentive to make a story, so they have incentive, perhaps, to over-crisisify" (Participant 25).

Whether or not the media exaggerate crises in higher education lies beyond the scope of this project, given that I intentionally interviewed higher education leaders and not the authors of the news articles who used the word "crisis" to describe the event or situation noted in their piece. However, these findings do highlight the provocative, suggestive, and at times attention-seeking qualities surrounding the discourse of crisis in higher education, whereby the decision to label something a crisis causes a reaction from various audiences that is more extreme, more emotional, more dramatic than the use of alternative words such as "incident," "problem," or "accident." Individuals with formal leadership authority in colleges and universities and media professionals who report on crisis situations are actively involved in amplifying, reifying, and disseminating messages surrounding these critical incidents facing institutions of higher education.

Previous experience with crises and crisis-like situations led many interviewees to comment on the emotional impact associated with this word. Crisis carries with it a set of underlying assumptions and impressions, leading one respondent to describe the baggage associated with this word: "Crisis has baggage. One of the things that we talked about very explicitly . . . we used to call it a 'crisis response plan.' And we recognized that the term 'crisis' had certain connotations that led people to not call, pick up the phone, and potentially activate our response plan because they're like, 'I'm not sure if this is a crisis. I don't want to make it bigger than it really is'" (Participant 12). This administrator went on to acknowledge that "we did very consciously recognize that the term crisis has baggage and creates a certain level of additional fear and concern that isn't necessarily always the best thing for addressing an issue that an institution of higher ed has to address" (Participant 12). As I continued with my interviews, the word "baggage" was repeated extensively by the participants, and it emerged as an in vivo code during the data analysis. When another senior administrator was asked to describe his experiences with crisis, he reiterated a widely acknowledged sentiment among the group—that the declaration of crisis invites immediate attention from internal and external audiences, which at times may be warranted, yet can also be disruptive or counterproductive: "I think if I were to say, 'we're in a crisis,' or the chancellor were to say, 'we're in a crisis,' that probably gets everybody's attention. We don't tend to use that word. I mean, you can probably find a whole bunch of stuff that we've said publicly, and I'd be surprised if we used the word very much . . . maybe because we're aware of the impact that it has" (Participant 15).

Within these moments of uncertainty, chaos, or trauma, attempts by leaders to manage the meaning of these critical incidents may involve deliberate efforts to characterize the event or situation as a crisis, and in doing so, others can more immediately share in this understanding. Put differently, the communicative behaviors of leaders have the very real potential to shape the conditions through which others interpret, respond to, and learn from any given situation. As a self-fulfilling prophecy, calling something a crisis can lead others to treat it as such. As one leader suggested, it is important for leaders in higher education to "validate people's concerns and help people feel comfortable in the university's response [to a crisis-like situation] . . . but also help de-escalate the situation so they don't feel like the sky is falling" (Participant 14). Crises imply "a sense of something being out of control . . . kind of a whiff of chaos" (Participant 17). Or, as another person offered, "it gives an implication of it being sort of the red alert or sirens sounding" (Participant 20). If we take seriously the idea of crisis as a social construction, we can begin to recognize the ways in which leaders use this label, the impact this labeling has on those directly and indirectly impacted by the critical moment under consideration, and the ways in which future "crises" might be perceived.

Conclusion

My conversations with senior higher education administrators have led me to more fully consider the ways in which crisis is both connected to some concrete reality and socially generated through communication. As noted by Estes (1983), "Crises are socially constructed as a consequence of social perception and definition; that is, a crisis may be said to exist if it is perceived to exist. By implication . . . a crisis does not exist if people do not act as though it exists" (p. 445).

Communication plays a fundamental role in the dynamics through which crises are shaped, and in some cases, created; and this theoretical grounding of crisis as a social construction provides a conceptual foundation upon which to further interrogate the emergence of and expectations for the practice of crisis leadership. To conclude, three primary themes regarding the social construction of crisis emerged from my interviews that may inform the treatment of crisis situations in higher education as both a focus of scholarly analysis and a domain of applied practice. First, if others perceive something to be a crisis, leaders would be wise to treat it as such. Second, leaders, through their rhetorical tools and formal and informal authority, may influence the perception of the crisis through acts of framing and meaning making, and with this authority come great opportunity and responsibility. Finally, the act of designating an event or series of events as a crisis by organizational leaders and the media often becomes a self-fulfilling prophecy, whereby talk of crisis heightens emotions, invites attention, and creates the conditions through which one experiences crisis-like situations.

The claims in this chapter support Hay's (1996) observation that "crisis, then is not some objective condition or property of a system defining the contours for subsequent ideological contestation. Rather, it is subjectively perceived and hence brought into existence through narrative and discourse" (p. 255). The combination of findings presented here leads to a depiction of crisis as a socially constructed, often subjective, and communicative phenomenon. Crises are thus understood to be incidents, events, or situations that present reputational risks and require immediate attention, and it is through communication and social interaction that they become crises. Crisis situations place unique demands on leaders that go beyond reputation management, and, as discussed in the next chapter, the ways in which crisis is defined can influence many of the leadership behaviors that accompany these types of events or situations.

Reflection Questions for Consideration

1. Do you tend to see crises as moments of danger that must be prevented or as unavoidable occasions for learning and improvement? What past experiences do you believe contributed to your perception of crisis?

2. Which of the models of crisis phases presented in this chapter resonated with you? In what ways might your understanding of the progression of crisis influence your approach to crisis prevention, management, and leadership?

3. Based on your reading of the social construction of crisis in the chapter, what concepts stand out as most important to you? How does this approach to understanding crisis align with your direct or indirect experiences of dealing with crisis situations? What elements of the social construction framework are most useful or most limiting?

3

The Process of Defining and Labeling Phenomena as Crises

Even a cursory review of the literature on crisis management makes it clear that the term "crisis" is subject to many definitions, and it is equally clear that the ways in which the term is defined may influence how crises are interpreted, classified, managed, and acted upon. This chapter explores the various definitions of crisis offered in the existing literature, along with various ways to analyze and make sense of the process through which these crises are identified and described. The impact of social media is also discussed in this chapter, in light of the dramatic influence these media have on the emergence and intensification of situations that are defined and labeled as crises. These perspectives will allow us, in the next chapter, to explore the taxonomy of crisis situations that are most germane to colleges and universities.

Defining Crisis: Common Concepts and Characteristics

The systematic study of crisis is a relatively young area. While crises have long been of interest, the tendency has been to write about and conceptualize them largely in an anecdotal and incident-specific manner. In their recent writing on the subject, Ulmer et al. (2018) describe the casual and often limited ways in which crisis is frequently discussed:

> Most likely, you will hear friends, fellow employees, or fellow students describe routine problems they are facing—fender benders, forgotten appointments, disgruntled mothers-in-law, bad hair days, or losing records of favorite university teams—as crises. All are bad experiences; however, they are not, by our definition, crises. Similarly, with some degree of regularity, organizations face events, such as unexpectedly low sales or the defection of key employees. Again, these are difficult times for organizations, but they are not necessarily crises. *Crises are unique moments in the history of organizations*. (P. 5; emphasis in original)

The widely praised response by Johnson & Johnson to the 1982 poisonings of Tylenol capsules, juxtaposed with the notoriously poor response to the *Exxon Valdez* oil spill in Prince William Sound in 1989, led to the emergence of the field of crisis management (Heath & O'Hair, 2009; Mitroff, 2004). Much of the writing on these cases focused on the individual crisis as an isolated event, paying specific attention to what happened, who was impacted, why the incident occurred, and what actions were taken in the short term and long term. These examples, along with more recent high-profile crises—such as the terrorist events on September 11, 2001, the devastation of Hurricane Katrina in 2005 or Hurricanes Maria, Irma, and Harvey in 2018, or the 2008 financial crisis, along with countless other examples—have each introduced new ways of thinking about the nature of crisis and the primary expectations for effectively managing *and* leading crisis situations. Only recently have efforts been made to develop more generalized understandings of the common elements and themes across multiple types of crises. There now exists a broad array of scholarly and professional literature committed to the study and practice of crisis management and crisis communication that provides numerous perspectives and definitions associated with the subject of crisis.

In an effort to advance a more wholistic framework for conceptualizing the broad array of potential crises, Ulmer et al. (2018) offer the following working definition that could account for a wide range of organizational crises: "An organizational crisis is a specific, *unexpected*, and *nonroutine* event or series of events that create high levels of *uncertainty* and simultaneously present an organization with both *opportunities* for and *threats* to its *high-priority goals*" (p. 7; emphasis in original). Their definition builds upon the work of Hermann (1963), who identified three characteristics of crisis— surprise, threat, and short response time. How one defines crisis often reflects the assumptions of a given situation, including one's perspective of the current state of affairs compared with the very possibilities of what an organization might become in the aftermath of the crisis (Mitroff, 2004).

Taking this broader perspective, crises can be characterized as events that have the potential to "disrupt the entire organization" (Pauchant & Mitroff, 1992, p. 3). Heath and Millar (2004) offer this description: "A crisis is typically defined as an untimely but predictable event that has actual or potential consequences for stakeholders' interests as well as the reputation of the organization suffering the crisis" (p. 2), which mirrors the definition put forth by Ruff and Aziz (2003): "any incident or situation, whether real, rumored or alleged, that can focus negative attention on a company or organization internally, in the media or before key audiences" (p. 3). Finally, it is worth acknowledging Fink's (1986) more balanced definition of the phenomenon as a "turning point, not necessarily laden with irreparable negativity but rather characterized by a certain degree of risk and uncertainty" (p. 23).

In considering these and other definitions found in the scholarly literature, several themes stand out.

- First, crisis has the potential to threaten the reputation and perceived status of the organization. Although it may also create an opportunity for learning, the moment or situation under scrutiny is understood to be a disruption from normal activity that may be problematic for the organization's short-term and long-term reputation (Irvine & Millar, 1998; Weick, 1988).
- Second, crisis requires an immediate response (Laermer, 2003; Mitroff, 2004). In the aftermath of a crisis, Ulmer et al. (2018) suggest the following postcrisis communication strategies: communicate early and often with both internal and external stakeholders; identify the cause of the crisis; contact everyone affected; and determine and communicate current and future risks (p. 38).
- Finally, the perception of internal and external stakeholders matters in moments of crisis (Benoit, 1995, 1997; Coombs, 2015; Mitroff, 2004). Beyond the direct and indirect impact on human lives, an added challenge for leaders during these periods of organizational vulnerability involves the ability to negotiate and make sense of the complexities of the crisis, while also responding in such a way as to maintain a favorable organizational reputation (Coombs & Holladay, 2005) and cultivate hope, trust, and safety for those one leads.

The threat to one's reputation, the centrality of communication, and the critical importance of how others perceive the organization coalesce in recent stakeholder-centered definitions of crisis advanced by a number of scholars (Coombs, 2007, 2018; Coombs & Holladay, 2002; Seeger & Sellnow, 2016; Stephens, Malone, & Bailey, 2005; Ulmer et al., 2018). For example, the communication perspective offered by Coombs (2015) addresses the importance of stakeholders, as stated in the following definition: "A crisis is the perception of an unpredictable event that threatens important expectancies of stakeholders and can seriously impact an organization's performance and generate negative outcomes" (p. 3). Diverse internal and external audiences are impacted by contemporary organizational crises, and at the same time, these very stakeholders are often actively involved in the generation and amplification of the crisis itself, particularly through their use of social media (Coombs, 2002; Heath, 1998; Pang, Nasrath, & Chong, 2014; Siah, Bansal, & Pang, 2010). The work on stakeholder theory (Freeman, 1984) presents a useful lens for examining the often conflicting interests, needs, values, and expectations of those who maintain a stake in the organization. As Lewis (2011) acknowledges, "Stakeholders enact the organization as the embodiment of their own purposes, their sense of how activities are related; how people are known; how outcomes arise and how processes unfold" (p. 6). Communication-centered definitions of crisis, therefore, must take into account the interests—and competing perceptions—of those who maintain a stake in the organization, of whom there are many in higher education (Ruben et al., 2017).

These definitions and perspectives have important implications for understanding the unique characterization of crisis in higher education. These themes are made prominent in Zdziarski's (2006) higher education–specific definition of crisis: "A crisis is an event, which is often sudden or unexpected, that disrupts the normal operations of the institution or its educational mission and threatens the well-being of personnel, property, financial resources, and/or reputation of the institution" (p. 3). My research on the subject, as described herein, has led me to identify the following working definition of "crisis":

> *events or situations of significant magnitude that threaten reputations, impact the lives of those involved in the institution, disrupt the ways in which the organization functions, have a cascading influence on leadership responsibilities and obligations across units/divisions, and require an immediate response from leaders.*

The multidimensional emphasis on reputational threat, communication, and stakeholder perception makes organizational crises both complex and compelling cases for leadership analysis.

Defining and Labeling Crisis Situations in Higher Education

To better understand the various crisis definitions and the process by which these crises become identified, described, and labeled as such, senior leaders in higher education were asked to consider the following questions: (1) What does the word "crisis" mean to you, thinking particularly about the context of higher education? (2) What factors/conditions play a role in treating a particular event or set of events as a crisis to which leaders must pay particular attention and respond? Several themes emerged from the data that directly address the defining and labeling of crises in higher education: (a) the multiple definitions of crisis; (b) crisis as distinct from other events or situations; and (c) the impact of social media in accelerating, accentuating, and escalating crises. The following is a discussion of these themes, along with a synthesis of illustrative quotes from the interviews that highlight them.

These definitions and perspectives on the topic of crisis in higher education varied in several respects and, at times, competed with one another. One leader suggested, "Oh, [crisis] could mean just about anything" (Participant 3); another offered, "You can argue that everything is a crisis" (Participant 1). Many of those interviewed for this project acknowledged that crises threaten reputations, impact the lives of those involved in the institution, and disrupt the ways in which the organization functions. Another individual noted, "I think that crisis is anything that has a significant impact on our student population, our staff and faculty population, the organizational reputation, and the ability for the organization to function and deliver the services to those groups" (Participant 8). As one administrator commented, a crisis is understood as "a problem that is significant . . . not a small problem, but a big problem that also has urgency associated with it" (Participant 15). Related to this idea, another respondent defined crisis as "the extreme end of risk" (Participant 19).

Based on their interview responses, senior leaders representing student affairs divisions seemed to have a higher and more specific threshold for classifying events as crises. As one vice president of Student Affairs shared:

Maybe it's the Student Affairs in me, but if no one's life is at risk, it's not truly a crisis. So I only categorize things as crisis if there's a threat to safety and if there's, you know, life at risk. Other than that, it's just a variation of steady-state chaos, and you know, there can be extra chaotic moments, like when you have a building takeover. And there can be more normative chaos, like when you're trying to deal with concerns about sexual misconduct, and concerns about race, and concerns about healthcare, and you know, trying to figure out how you're gonna finance something . . . those are more steady-state chaos, so, I think higher ed is now just degrees of chaos. And crisis is when it crosses over into threat to life. (Participant 19)

Many of the Student Affairs representatives shared this sentiment that the "crisis" label was reserved for only the most severe cases, particularly those situations where lives are threatened. For example, one individual described crises as "the catastrophic things" (Participant 13), and, as another noted, "Usually you are not getting a phone call 9 to 5 dealing with a crisis, it's usually later in the evening or after midnight" (Participant 32). Suggesting that leaders in Student Affairs "deal with crises . . . on almost a daily basis unfortunately" (Participant 9), the data indicate that this subgroup of respondents tended to exercise caution when using the label "crisis" to describe situations of lesser magnitude.

One additional idea to emerge from the interview data with regard to multiple definitions of crisis reflected the ways in which organizational crisis disrupts, violates, and threatens the mission of the college or university. For example, one respondent noted, "I think of crises as anything that pulls us away from the work of the mission of the institution in a way that could lead to damage, reputationally or otherwise to the institution" (Participant 1). The importance of mission was noted by another administrator: "Bottom line is, [crises] are things that disrupt the core mission of the university in one way or another" (Participant 29). Speaking of the core services of an institution, a senior leader offered the following definition: "I guess [a crisis] would be an issue that surfaces that affects the trust or the value of what the institution is meant to deliver for people. It potentially calls into question the institution's ability to provide educational or research or service support or protection or safety in the course of doing its work" (Participant 20). Several respondents also referred to those events or situations that threaten the university's ability to fulfill its core mission(s) in the service of its primary stakeholders, while causing people to "potentially think poorly of the institution's management of that situation" (Participant 28).

The interview data shared in this section point to the varying ways in which administrators perceive crisis in higher education, yet there is much agreement that crisis cuts at the core of the institution. This disruption, violation, or threat to the mission of the college or university has direct and indirect impacts on multiple internal and external audiences, which can also influence the perceptions of the institution's reputation, unlike incidents of a lesser degree of peril that are explored in the following section.

CRISIS AS DISTINCT FROM OTHER EVENTS OR SITUATIONS

The differentiation of crisis from nuisance, problem, challenge, or incident was another important theme to emerge in the interviews. Leaders across higher education must take seriously the possibilities for crisis on their campuses and in the environment, and as the following comments indicate, part of the challenge involves separating potential crisis situations from other events that are more localized in scope. Isolated incidents, minor nuisances, and intermittent disruptions in process or protocol certainly require careful attention, as they always have the potential to rise to the level of crisis, especially when these matters become more frequent or complex in scope and scale. Too much time focused on these smaller affairs, however, can distract leaders from the more significant matters that demand their attention.

As suggested by one senior leader, "Not every crisis that people have needs to be a crisis or should be a crisis.

Sometimes people think they're in crisis and they're really not, because if you've got three months to figure out something it's not a crisis, it's a job" (Participant 36). Another senior administrator from University Communications who is responsible for working with individual departments that encounter situations that might rise to the level of crisis offered the following example: "Somebody in our Health Center might think of something as a crisis. It might damage the reputation of a program or maybe even an individual, and those are things to be dealt with, but they don't rise to the level of a true crisis in my opinion. We get this all the time with people who think there's a major crisis going on, but the reality is, once we dig into it, it's really not. It's more of a nuisance, and there's a big difference between a nuisance and a crisis" (Participant 5). Many of the interview responses also differentiated "crisis" from "problem," "incident," or "challenge." As explained by one senior Finance and Business leader, "We face challenges every day. Not all challenges reach crisis proportions" (Participant 10). He went on to suggest the following: "To me, some things become a true crisis when it threatens health and safety of people that work on or visit the campus, when it threatens the institution's reputation, when it threatens the institution's financial well-being or stability" (Participant 10). Additionally, when describing her experience with campus sexual assaults or suicide, another administrator offered the following observation: "Generally, when there's more than one [incident] we move into crisis mode. When there's a singular incident, it's an incident. When they become multiple, it becomes a crisis" (Participant 1). This distinction was summarized similarly by another leader: "An individual's suicide is an incident we need to attend to, but it is not going to affect the whole campus. But when you have a string of them—like, I'm thinking back to the situation up at Cornell a few years ago when you had folks jumping [from bridges into gorges]—and it reaches an issue of severe magnitude and it's likely to impact the entire campus, and the reputation of the institution, then I think you've got a crisis" (Participant 21).

THE IMPACT OF SOCIAL MEDIA IN ACCELERATING, ACCENTUATING, AND ESCALATING CRISES

In addition to offering multiple definitions of crises—events or situations perceived to be different from isolated incidents or emergencies—the influence of social media was discussed by nearly every administrator I interviewed. It is clear from these responses that an understanding of the nature of crisis in colleges and universities must consider the increasingly significant role of social media in accelerating, accentuating, and escalating events to the level of crisis. One leader noted, "I think it's just very clear that the world that we all operate in has changed dramatically. Things that ten or certainly fifteen years ago would have flown under the radar screen, now because of the omnipresence of digital devices . . . anybody can become a quasi-journalist" (Participant 10). Some administrators attributed the perceived increase in crisis situations to the rise of social media. Characterizing social media as a "mixed blessing" (Participant 17), many respondents generally acknowledged its value as a mechanism through which institutions and their leaders can monitor and quickly respond to these incidents; yet, despite this opportunity, the respondents also addressed the public availability of information and misinformation through social media that is both "emotional and visceral" (Participant 12). Respondents also highlighted the ways in which social media have complicated the role of and the expectations placed on the senior administrator in higher education.

According to participants, through the use of social media, both information and misinformation can travel "like wildfire" (Participant 26), leading to a "multiplier effect" (Participant 22) whereby much of the content is rapidly distributed, yet not "necessarily grounded in fact" (Participant 30). For example, as described by one senior Finance and Business leader, "We have to be sensitive to the fact that issues or challenges can escalate much, much more rapidly. Disgruntled employees can take to Twitter or send something off to any one of a number of different social media sites, and all of a sudden, something that seemed small can escalate dramatically" (Participant 18). Another Student Affairs leader described the experience of a colleague who observed phones lighting up across the audience while sitting on the platform of a commencement ceremony. "It turned out that a student committed suicide fifteen minutes before and no one in the administration knew because it happened so quickly. . . . Basically, the entire campus knew about it and was talking about it before the administration even knew of it" (Participant 35). In addition to allowing for the rapid dissemination of news, "the electronic communication that's available now means that you're just getting advice and condemnation and excoriation from all quarters" (Participant 15).

Several administrators described social media as both a blessing and a curse (Participants 17 and 35) for leaders in higher education. Respondents spoke of the advantages of using social media to both monitor stakeholder attitudes and respond swiftly to multiple audiences, including those with whom institutions may not have had strong relationships before. One senior leader representing University Relations described the importance of social media "as a pretty good barometer and leading edge of what you might see soon" (Participant 27). Put another way, another administrator suggested that "nothing is local, everything is interconnected. . . . I have to be aware of what's happening anywhere because it's inevitable through social media that we will be influenced by it" (Participant 19). Institutional presence in this digital space is critical, and as one respondent representing University Communications suggested, the technology allows leaders to "be aware of what people are saying, but you're trying to answer their concerns there also" (Participant 17). Within the national context of widespread racial tension and campus unrest, for example, several administrators described their personal experience of responding to emergent challenges via social media. In one widely discussed example, "students started a hashtag about their perceptions of what it was like to be a student of color here [where] they posted about difficult experiences that they have been having. Typically, we try to at least be [digitally] present. We certainly are always monitoring; but in a case like that, we had some senior administrators who at least posted in that hashtag just to say, 'We're here. We are listening. We are trying to learn from your experiences'" (Participant 17).

Another administrator from the same institution described the dilemma of how best to respond to this unfolding situation: "We had to weigh in on it, but we had to express our sympathy and understanding of what was being conveyed. One of the things that we debated is, do we talk about this in a general way or do we talk about specifically this hashtag?" (Participant 25). The available technology allows leaders to monitor the digital conversation and respond accordingly, "in the channels that people are consuming. Meet people where they are" (Participant 25).

The escalation of incidents or situations to the status of crisis through social media was described by many using terms such as "blow up" (Participant 23), "catch fire faster" (Participant 25), "get really like wildfire" (Participant 16), "become caught in a firestorm" (Participant 3), and "explode" (Participant 31). As one interviewee described it, "Depending on how the situation is viewed and the amount of traction on social media, this could either blow up and be a crisis or this could largely pass" (Participant 23). According to the senior leaders in this study, the challenge for all institutions, including institutions of higher education, is to embrace new technology to monitor stakeholder attitudes and use the available technology to communicate quickly and frequently with these key audiences. Crises drive people to social media for additional information, and it is also through social media that certain crises emerge. One respondent described this as follows: "We need to have a more sophisticated set of monitoring tools to understand [how information spreads]. If it 'catches fire' at 10:30 at night in a dorm and grows through a social community there, and we wait until 10:00 A.M. the next morning to realize that it happened before weighing in, a huge amount of perception has already been shaped" (Participant 25). This is particularly challenging for institutions of higher education, as supported by several research participants, "because our institutions are not built to respond to that, nor do we really have the right monitoring infrastructure" (Participant 25). Numerous administrators described the importance of investing in an appropriate technical infrastructure, including some type of available social media monitoring software, and gaining the necessary expertise to better deal with the challenges posed by social media, particularly its role in the elevation of incidents to the level of crisis.

Many of those interviewed also described the impact of social media on their work as leaders more generally. The immediacy of social media sets up leaders for failure, as one administrator noted, because "we can't do it as timely as people want" (Participant 9). Reflecting on the evolution of technology, one administrator explained, "Social media has made every movement international . . . and social media also means there's no air time. You know, I often comment that thirty-five years ago when we had an incident . . . there were going to be a couple of days before anyone really knew about it" (Participant 19). Several interviewees shared specific strategies that their president/chancellor or they personally use to communicate during crises through social media; however, as one chancellor candidly admitted, "I know next to nothing about [social media]. We have people who are dealing with that stuff" (Participant 28). Finally, recognizing the rapid change and excessive expectations associated with the role of social media in addressing crises, one senior leader confessed, "I have moments where I'm glad I'm as old I am, because I don't know that if I had twenty-five years left doing this that I would be able to make it with the power of social media—the way people communicate today" (Participant 34). Whether this sentiment is widespread among senior leaders in higher education is unknown, although the findings from these interviews indicate a very strong relationship between the increased scrutiny of higher education and its leaders and the increasingly pervasive role of social media.

Conclusion

The ideas presented in this chapter underscore the multiple, and often conflicting, definitions of crises, and the ways that senior leaders in higher education differentiate crises from incidents, nuisances, or problems, depending on their magnitude and severity. Additionally, the process of defining and labeling events as crises is further complicated by the pervasive role of social media in accelerating, accentuating, and elevating events to the symbolic level of crisis through the rapid dissemination of information and misinformation. To refer back to the working definition of crisis in this book, crises—particularly those that impact or have the potential to impact colleges and universities—are events or situations of significant magnitude that threaten reputations, impact the lives of those involved in the institution, disrupt the ways in which the organization functions, have a cascading influence on leadership responsibilities and obligations across units/divisions, and require an immediate response from leaders. By approaching the study of organizational crisis through a communicative lens, we are able to consider the stakeholder's active role in socially constructing crises and the direct and indirect impact of these events on multiple audiences and organizational reputations.

One might argue that there are different communicative assumptions that lead one to distinguish a nuisance, problem, challenge, or incident from that which is labeled a "true crisis" (Participant 5). The differences, as depicted in the findings from the interviews, may involve scope of impact, urgency, or frequency. These findings are consistent with the descriptions of crisis as a social construction, as offered in Estes (1983) and Schultz and Raupp (2010). Specifically, "the term crisis implies that the event or condition so described is different from others" (Estes, 1983, p. 446), and the labeling of the event or condition as a crisis contributes to the construction of the situation itself—and the ways in "which actors react to and make sense of the crisis" (Schultz & Raupp, 2010).

The many definitions of crisis raised in my conversations with the various senior leaders parallel many of the definitions found in the existing scholarly literature. In regard to the ways in which crisis is defined, one administrator shared that "the definition of a crisis is one that I think is a little bit fluid and evolves, as does the management and response to it" (Participant 18). Two different administrators paraphrased the colloquial expression made famous by U.S. Supreme Court Justice Potter Stewart in his 1964 description of his threshold test for obscenity: "It's kind of like you know [crisis] when you see it" (Participant 30). The social construction of crisis involves more than "seeing it," "defining it," and "knowing it." Through communication, the social construction of crisis involves "calling it" a crisis, which then sets into motion a series of implications for the practice of crisis leadership. Therefore, an exploration into the ways in which crisis is both defined and labeled becomes both an important conceptual exercise and a strategic leadership exercise for those with formal and informal influence in higher education.

Reflection Questions for Consideration

1. If you were to ask colleagues and family members to define a crisis, what words or themes would they tend to emphasize in their definitions? In what ways do these definitions shape how one thinks about, reacts to, and learns from crisis situations?

2. Reread the definition of crisis provided in this chapter: Crisis is an event or situation of significant magnitude that threatens reputations, impacts the lives of those involved in the institution, disrupts the ways in which the organization functions, has a cascading influence on leadership responsibilities and obligations across units/divisions, and requires an immediate response from leaders. Which elements of this definition are most or least connected with your experience with or understanding of crises?

3. In what ways have social media accelerated, accentuated, and escalated events to the level of crisis at your institution? What aspects of social media and new technology do you find most useful for effectively leading in crisis? What aspects of social media and new technology would you expect to be most problematic for leading in crisis?

4

The Characterization and Categorization of Crises in Higher Education

Colleges and universities are in many ways unique, unlike other types of organizations. The multiple and sometimes blurry purpose(s)/mission(s), structural complexity, extensive array of stakeholders and cultures, and tradition of shared governance are some of the components that distinguish colleges and universities from other sectors (Ruben & Gigliotti, 2017a; Ruben et al., 2017). If we understand crises to be socially constructed phenomena—events or situations of significant magnitude that are perceived by stakeholders to threaten reputations, impact the lives of those involved in the institution, disrupt the ways in which the organization functions, have a cascading influence on leadership responsibilities and obligations across units/divisions, and require an immediate response from leaders—there is much to learn by focusing on the types of crises that are most germane to colleges and universities. However, as suggested elsewhere, the temptation to view colleges and universities as unique can also be limiting, for in many ways, colleges and universities—and their constituent units and departments—share much in common with other sectors and other organizations (Ruben & Gigliotti, 2017a). As detailed in this chapter, because many of these crisis types are not wholly distinctive to institutions of higher education, college and university leaders can benefit from cross-institutional learning as a way of studying the types of crises other sectors face and the ways in which their leaders approach these issues of significance.

Overview of Crisis Taxonomies

In addition to the diverse assortment of definitions of crisis in the existing literature, also extant in the literature is a variety of categories of crises that college and university leaders may one day encounter, such as natural disasters, technical breakdowns, and incidents of violence. As illustrated in table 4.1, the scholarly literature includes numerous crisis taxonomies (Gigliotti & Fortunato, 2017), many of which distinguish man-made crises from natural disasters that lie beyond the control of human influence (Lindell, Prater, & Perry, 2007). All colleges and universities have protocols and policies in place for dealing with inclement weather, cyberattacks, or active shooters. As other types of crises become more common, leaders in higher education are beginning to plan and prepare for alternative types of situations that have risen to the level of crisis at other institutions, such as visits by controversial speakers, widespread protests surrounding racial unrest, and inflammatory verbal statements and social media posts by students, faculty, and staff.

Effective crisis leadership in higher education requires individuals to consider the wide array of crisis events or situations that might affect the institution, take appropriate measures to prevent certain crises, and carefully plan and prepare for the impact of these potential crises. Looking at the list of crisis types detailed in table 4.1, in what ways can

TABLE 4.1. Crisis Taxonomies

LERBINGER (1997)

• Natural	• Technological
• Confrontation	• Malevolence
• Skewed management values	• Deception
• Management misconduct	• Business and economic

MEYERS & HOLUSHA (1986)

• Public perception	• Sudden market shifts	• Product failure
• Top management succession	• Cash crises	• Industrial relations crises
• Hostile takeover	• Adverse international events	• Regulation/deregulation

COOMBS, HAZELTON, HOLLIDAY, & CHANDLER (1995)

• Natural disasters	• Human breakdowns
• Technical breakdowns	• Organizational misdeeds
• Challenges	• Rumors
• Workplace violence	
• Malevolence	

MITROFF & ANAGNOS (2001)

• Economic	• Informational	• Natural disasters
• Human resource	• Reputation	• Psychopathic acts
• Physical loss of key plants and other facilities		

COOMBS (2007)

Victim Crises: Minimal Responsibility	*Accident Crises: Low Responsibility*	*Preventable Crises: Strong Responsibility*
• Natural disasters	• Challenges	• Human-error accidents
• Rumors	• Technical-error accidents	• Human-error product harm
• Workplace violence	• Technical-error product harm	• Organizational misdeeds
• Product tampering / malevolence		

leadership teams adequately plan for the range of financial, legal, and reputational crises that might emerge? Zdziarski, Rollo, and Dunkel (2007) introduce a useful conceptual model—what they refer to as a "crisis matrix"—that leaders in higher education may consult to assess crisis, determine the impact of the event or situation on the campus community, and identify alternatives for best responding to the crisis. Their crisis matrix consists of three dimensions: the level of crisis (e.g., critical incident, campus emergency, and disaster), the type of crisis (e.g., environmental crises, facility crises, and human crises), and perceived intentionality of crisis (e.g., unintentional and intentional crises). According to the authors of the model, "Every event, no matter how it concludes, starts as a critical incident. The scale, scope, and impact are what expand the incident through the matrix, absorbing new constituencies, requiring additional resources, and affecting the ability to respond" (p. 43). The crisis types identified as most salient for higher education, as detailed in the pages ahead, can be incorporated into this conceptual model as leaders plan for, respond to, and learn from these important "crucible moments" (Bennis & Thomas, 2002).

An Exploration into Contemporary Crises in Higher Education

Of little surprise to current college and university leaders, higher education is the subject of much national and international media attention and public scrutiny. This is due, in part, to the many stakeholders who have an interest in higher education, many of whom maintain competing perceptions of the role of postsecondary education. Additionally, as discussed in Ruben et al. (2017), the high level of scrutiny is the result of two intersecting public perceptions: first, education beyond high school is recognized as critical in our current knowledge economy, and, second, higher education is unreasonably expensive. I would offer a third explanation for the increased focus on and scrutiny of higher education. Colleges and universities, unlike many other sectors, are held in high regard by many for their noble mission(s), aspirational purpose(s), and ambitious core values. Colleges and universities are trusted to make decisions that are in the best interest of the students who call our institutions home and of the larger public who benefit from our research, programs, and services. As former president of Wellesley College and Duke University Nannerl Keohane (2006) writes, "Colleges and universities play a crucial part in determining whether humanity will indeed have a future, and what it will be like. Our institutions have significant moral purposes; we are not just collections of loosely affiliated persons with convergent or conflicting interests, but institutions that make a difference in the world through pursuing our basic goals" (p. 2). When leaders fail to model behaviors that are consistent with this moral purpose, particularly in the public spotlight of high-stakes crisis situations, public trust and confidence can become slowly eroded, a topic to which I will return later in this book.

Prior to interviewing senior college and university leaders for this project, I was first interested in gathering data on the ways in which crisis was characterized in the news coverage of higher education. A content analysis of higher education news outlets from 2011 to 2015, including the *Chronicle of Higher Education* and *Inside Higher Ed*, resulted in the identification of 983 articles that included the word "crisis" or "crises" within the title or body of the article.

A content analysis of forty-eight of the most recent articles from the *New York Times* and eight articles from the *Wall Street Journal*, all of which referred to some type of "crisis" in higher education, resulted in consistent types of events

TABLE 4.2. Breakdown of Coded Articles by Year

YEAR	NUMBER OF ARTICLES	PERCENTAGE
2011	225	23
2012	264	27
2013	173	19
2014	132	13
2015	189	19
Total Number	**983**	**101**[a]

[a]Due to rounding.

such as those found in the higher education news outlets. I reviewed the smaller sample of articles from these two news outlets to ensure that the events or situations characterized as crises in these mainstream outlets were included in the more extensive search of articles in the *Chronicle of Higher Education* and *Inside Higher Ed*. See Table 4.2 for a breakdown of articles by year.

I was also interested in classifying who used the label "crisis" to describe the event, situation, or series of events presented in the news article, and those results are given in table 4.3. The criteria detailed in table 4.3 emerged from a two-stage coding process. First, I identified the individuals who used the "crisis" label in the various articles; and second, to simplify and identify patterns, these were combined into the more general categories presented in the table. As evidenced by the data, these findings suggest that in an overwhelming number of cases (832 of 1,005), the authors of the news write-up took the liberty of describing the event or series of events as a crisis. For example, writing about reactions to the initial closing of Sweet Briar College, Kolowich (2015) wrote the following: "Why were the alumnae hearing about the college's existential crisis only now, after the decision to close was already made?" In other cases, a wide array

TABLE 4.3. Summary of Use of the "Crisis" Label

SOURCE	NUMBER OF ARTICLES
Author of the article	832
Administrative leader within the college or university facing the crisis	29
Administrative leader from another college or university in response to the crisis	3
Internal stakeholder (e.g., student, alumnus, faculty member, board member) who is directly or indirectly impacted by the crisis	68
External stakeholder (e.g., National Collegiate Athletic Association, accrediting agency, parent) who is directly or indirectly impacted by the crisis	73
Total Number[a]	1,005

[a] Note that the total exceeds the full number of articles in the sample, as there were several instances where more than one individual described the event as a crisis, including instances where the author both independently used the label and cited an internal or external stakeholder who declared the event a crisis.

of internal or external stakeholders (173 of the total) were quoted as describing the situation as a crisis. For example, in response to racial tensions at the University of Kansas, Brown (2015) described the response from a group of internal stakeholders: "The senate's executive committee saw the two leaders' alleged indifference as a sign that neither 'has the intention of responding to the crisis our black peers face on this campus.'" Although this research method does not allow us to consider the motivations for why individuals used the "crisis" label, the findings seem to suggest that the authors of the news articles liberally invoke the term in their writing on higher education. Additionally, based on the available evidence from this sample, the findings of this content analysis indicate that senior leaders are far less likely than other internal or external stakeholders to use the "crisis" label in their public characterization of an event or series of events.

In addition to the empirical evidence offered in the tables, the findings from this analysis also addressed three themes that will be discussed in the forthcoming sections. The types of crises described in the news coverage surrounding higher education reflect multiple categories, classified across three dimensions (i.e., domain, responsibility, and declaration), with the impact often distributed across numerous divisions and units. An understanding of the types of crises that are most likely to affect colleges and universities can help leaders most effectively anticipate and prepare for the challenges and obstacles that may lie ahead. Furthermore, as will be discussed, these findings help to explain what makes the practice of crisis leadership in higher education a particularly complex and multifaceted endeavor.

Multiple Categories of Relevant Crises in Higher Education

Upon counting the frequency of certain crisis examples in the selected news stories, I classified the types of crises that were most widely acknowledged in the media using an existing taxonomy of crisis categories developed by Mitroff, Diamond, and Alpaslan (2006), which underwent refinements as this project progressed. This taxonomy by Mitroff et al. initially provided me with a baseline set of crisis examples that were most prevalent for institutions of higher education, the results of which are displayed in table 4.4.

These findings point to a significantly high incidence of financial-oriented crises during this particular time period, as compared to the other crisis types; however, almost 400 of the coded examples could not be appropriately classified using this existing taxonomy.

When it became apparent that the classification scheme was limited and not entirely well aligned with the emerging

TABLE 4.4. Results Using the Mitroff, Diamond, and Alpaslan (2006) Coding Scheme

CODE	NUMBER	PERCENTAGE
Criminal: rapes/murders/robberies/guns/gangs/ terrorism	41	4
Informational/technological: identity theft/violations of confidentiality/ fraud	2	<1
Building safety	1	<1
Athletics: recruiting practices / academic, hazing, or sex scandals	54	5
Unethical behavior/misconduct: fraud/plagiarism/ record tampering/conflicts of interest	6	<1
Financial	398	40
Natural disaster	14	1
Legal/labor disputes and academic employment issues (adjuncts, part-time lecturers, etc.)	71	7
Perceptual/reputational: false rumors/stories	13	1
Other	384	39
Total	984	100

and increasing number of crisis incidents found in the more recent news coverage, a more general taxonomy was created for the purposes of this study. This revised taxonomy, provided in table 4.5, includes the crisis type, some examples offered by one or more of the senior administrators interviewed in this study, and an illustrative quote that highlights the crisis type. Several of the crisis categories from the Mitroff et al. (2006) taxonomy also appeared in the revised taxonomy (e.g., athletics, natural disaster, financial); however, the revised taxonomy also included a number of more general categories that initially were not present (e.g., academic, facilities, student affairs). This comprehensive taxonomy of crisis types in higher education accounted for all of the crisis examples detailed in the search of news articles, and I also confirmed that the types of crises described in each of my interviews with senior administrators were represented in this broader taxonomy.

TABLE 4.5. Taxonomy of Crisis Types in Higher Education

CRISIS TYPE	EXAMPLE	ILLUSTRATIVE QUOTE
Academic crisis	Debate over tenure; widespread plagiarism or academic fraud; significant violations of academic integrity	"Of all the things that have happened, one of the elements of it that really did feel like a crisis was when an employee of the university publicly stated that we have been accepting students that couldn't read, so that put us more into crisis mode just more than anything else that happened during that period of time." (Participant 15)
Athletics crisis	Athlete hazing incidents; child abuse scandals	"I would tell you candidly that when the Sandusky crisis hit this institution in November 2011, I think it's fair to say Penn State was not well prepared to deal with or respond to a crisis of that magnitude. There was, I think, a fair amount of fumbling and indecisiveness that went on. In some cases, indecisiveness actually rendered decisions that were, in hindsight, regrettable. It's one of those things where if you had a do-over, you might approach some of these things a bit differently. [As] we dealt with some of the ensuing waves of events, like the release of the Freeh Report and the nationwide reaction to that, followed quickly by the sanctions that were imposed by the NCAA, it was clear that we remained in a full-blown crisis response mode." (Participant 10)
Clinical crisis	Physician malpractice in academic health center	N/A
Technological crisis	Cyberattack	"One is at a very basic level, a crisis means that you have an online service or you know, one of our critical technological tools is not available. To have a tool like, you know, HR system, or even our main webpage, you know, not be up and available for people to see or to use, in our world is the crisis. And the second area, which leads kinda to the first, is you know, the information security, cyber security kinds of activities and threats that we continually grapple with which can lead to a disruption of a service, but also can lead to, you know, inappropriate access to information assets at the university, so those kinds of events we treat as crises as well." (Participant 26)

Facilities crisis	Water main break; chemical spill; widespread power outage; significant damage to university infrastructure	"We had a chemical spill in a chemistry/engineering lab. I get a call at dinner with my family at 8 o'clock at night and somebody had reported it." (Participant 22)
Financial or business crisis	Significant decreases in state appropriations	"For every school, and certainly some of the large publics with significant decreases in state appropriations, depending on whether you're a Research 1 institution that receives external funding from NIH. Of course, market commissions, all of those types of things, are putting enormous pressure on institutions of higher education. I think you could potentially label it as a financial crisis. I don't think it takes on the same type of communication or the same types of protocols [as other crises], but you are looking at financial issues that then run through the entire operation. It's looking at all of your costs, so are you able to run the operation in a more efficient and a less costly way, which leads to all kinds of interesting conversations around outsourcing the size of the workforce, including the faculty, conversations about distance education, all of those types of issues." (Participant 18)
Human resources crisis	Employee crimes, issues surrounding hiring and firing of employees	"One of the areas of crisis that our office deals with is when there's a very public faculty misconduct issue. We had one year where we had three faculty felons. Those became very public because in one case it was a faculty member who was allegedly trying to entice a fourteen-year-old on the Internet or criminal stalking. Those became issues that normally we would deal with faculty misconduct in a fairly private manner, investigation on campus, conclusion that there was misappropriation of funds, scientific research misconduct. When it gets elevated because it's part of the public discourse in the news media, that becomes a crisis that we have to deal with. That's probably the big one." (Participant 12)
Leadership or governance crisis	Conflict between state legislature and university leadership	"I think the one's that's sort of the most corrosive for the place like long-term is the fact that the governor and the legislature are coming at higher education from a different direction than this institution. I mean, that's difficult because our funding depends on it. Our tenure depends on it. So many certain vital elements. We're a state agency." (Participant 17)

(continued)

TABLE 4.5. (Continued)

CRISIS TYPE	EXAMPLE	ILLUSTRATIVE QUOTE
Natural disaster	Flood, tornado, or hurricane	"The University of Iowa had its 'Flood of the Century' back in '93. It was a 100-year flood. It hit the campus hard. The water overflowed the Coralville Reservoir. That's upstream from us, and it took out a number of buildings, and I think damaged the buildings, the campus back in '93, dollars I think was the $6 million range, maybe $10 million, and was something that was never going to be forgotten by those who experienced that. Then fast forward fifteen years later to '08, when we started seeing the water coming and getting those early warnings that we could be dealing with another flood, it was interesting to see that half this organization, facilities or half the campus for that matter, were going around and saying, 'My God, this could be as bad as '93,' and were doing things based on their experience in '93. The other half of us, and I joined the campus in '03, had no reference of it or experience with that. In a way, that experience of '93 limited people to the scale of what this could become. They couldn't imagine it being as bad as it was in '93. We were many times worse. The rest of us weren't encumbered by that reference point, so to speak. We didn't know what '93 was and we were just ... Boy. It was just fun to see some folks reacting to a previous disaster and others reacting to the current disaster. One of my ten lessons learned that I always had down is plan for your next disaster, not your last one." (Participant 11)

Public safety crisis	Active shooter; sexual assault; suicide; or death	"I say that that [the Virginia Tech massacre] was like the 9/11 of higher education, that mass shooting. When there's thirty-two people killed by a shooter, that's about as horrible as things get." (Participant 30)
Racial or identity conflict	Campus unrest due to racial or identity tensions within the community and acts of intolerance by any campus stakeholder	"There were certainly a lot of crises across college campuses this past year because people underreacted to the situation at hand. You saw that with the racial tensions at Missouri, a really good example I think....As the leader not addressing it, not being transparent about it, not meeting it head on, and therefore the perception was: you don't care about this. It doesn't matter whether it's right or wrong. You don't care about it, and that just escalated the whole thing. You have an underreaction which caused an escalation." (Participant 27)
Student affairs crisis	Mental health crisis	"I think that students' mental health is a major concern. I think it continues to be a growing concern. We are seeing that more students are coming forward, and so I don't know if that is because of a removal of stigma or if it's because many students have already, previous to coming to campus, have had interactions with mental health professionals....but I do know that we are seeing more students." (Participant 24)

Complexity and Crosscutting Nature of Crisis

An examination of the events and situations characterized as crises in the selected news stories, along with a review of the aggregate of coded articles, led to the development of a more general crisis classification scheme as shown in table 4.6. This more inclusive classification taxonomy provided a useful scheme through which to explore the complexity and crosscutting nature of crises in higher education, as found in both the content analysis and interview data for this study.

Specifically, the coded articles from the content analysis clustered primarily around three emergent themes: crisis domain, crisis responsibility, and crisis declaration. Based on the content analysis, it became important and useful to differentiate between two different crisis domains, *institutional* and *environmental*. From the analysis of media coverage, it also became apparent that the leadership responsibility for dealing with the crisis often varied from *one specific unit or division* of the institution to those crises that have an *interdependent influence on multiple units or divisions*. It was also necessary to distinguish the declaration of crisis based on those that are *self-declared* by internal stakeholders within an institution from those that are *other-declared* by external stakeholders outside of the institution. This classification scheme, depicted in table 4.6, provides a brief description of these emergent themes, along with relevant examples from the content analysis that illustrate each of these themes.[1]

Varied Scope of Impact

A final theme to emerge from this part of my study that can inform how leaders in higher education navigate the contested nature of crisis relates directly to the scope of the impact triggered by the event or situation. I initially set out

TABLE 4.6. Crisis Classification Scheme

EMERGENT THEMES AND SUBTHEMES	DESCRIPTION	EXAMPLES
Crisis Domain • **Institutional crises** • **Environmental crises**	There are notable differences between institutional crises and environmental crises.	**Institutional crises** (e.g., school shooting, allegations of fraud, student death, campus protests at one particular college or university) **Environmental crises** (e.g., broader issues in the higher education environment that present challenges to the larger system, including the crisis in the humanities, the crisis in legal education, the financial crisis in higher education, and the student loan crisis)
Crisis Responsibility • **One unit or division** • **Multiple units or divisions**	The leadership responsibility for dealing with the crisis often varies from **one specific unit or division of the institution** to those crises that have an **interdependent influence on multiple units or divisions.**	**One specific unit or division of the institution** (e.g., leaders in technology services are primarily responsible for dealing with a cyberattack that impacts the institution; leaders in student affairs are often responsible for addressing issues of hazing in the fraternity and sorority community) **Interdependent influence on multiple units or divisions** (e.g., sudden and significant decreases in freshman enrollment become the responsibility of leaders in enrollment services, the business office, academic services, and student services; damage due to hurricanes has a direct impact on the facilities, human resources, and business operations of a college or university; campus sexual assaults require primary attention from leaders in both human resources and student affairs; and the emergence of an active shooter will have a rippling effect across all divisional units)

(continued)

TABLE 4.6. (Continued)

EMERGENT THEMES AND SUBTHEMES	DESCRIPTION	EXAMPLES
Crisis Declaration • **Self-declared** • **Other-declared**	The invocation of crisis may be **self-declared** by internal stakeholders within an institution or **other-declared** by external stakeholders outside of the institution.	**Self-Declared** In response to racial tensions at the University of Kansas, Brown (2015) described the response from a group of internal stakeholders: "The senate's executive committee saw the two leaders' alleged indifference as a sign that neither 'has the intention of responding to the crisis our black peers face on this campus.'" **Other-Declared** As Kolowich (2015) wrote with regard to the closing of Sweet Briar College, "Why were the alumnae hearing about the college's existential crisis only now, after the decision to close was already made?"

to code the articles based on the extent of the impact of the declared crisis, ranging from limited impact to one division of the institution (e.g., Student Affairs, Business/Financial Operations, Academic Affairs, Athletics) to university-wide impact. In some instances, when writing about a particular crisis, the author of the news article may have emphasized the role of one specific college or university division in addressing the crisis at hand, and there were some clear-cut situations that were directly aligned with one division of the institution over another (e.g., leaders in Academic Affairs were most directly impacted by issues related to academic integrity; leaders in Athletics were most affected by a hazing situation involving one of the sports teams). However, the content analysis revealed that the process of responding to, managing, and leading during crisis situations was often much more complex, multifaceted, and interdependent, with primary decision-making authority and potential impact distributed across numerous divisions and units. As explained by one of the senior leaders with whom I spoke, "I think once you become a vice president, you become an institutional officer and your purview is not just your portfolio. So, like when we had this racist, misogynist e-mail, that wasn't just a student affairs problem, that was a campus-wide problem" (Participant 21). In many instances, it became apparent that, unlike isolated incidents that might limit the impact to one unit or department, a crisis in higher education has the potential to impact the reputation and operations of an entire institution, with responsibility often distributed across multiple divisions and units.

Conclusion

As detailed in this first half of the book, the complexity and scope of crises in higher education are becoming increasingly clear. First, crises appear to be socially constructed, often subjective, and communicative phenomena that require the attention of leaders. Next, crises are subject to multiple, and often conflicting, definitions, and the process of defining and labeling events as crises is complicated by many factors, such as the distinct mission(s), multiple stakeholders, and unique organizational components associated with institutions of higher education, along with the pervasive role of social media in accelerating, accentuating, and elevating events to the symbolic level of crisis through the spread of information and misinformation. Finally, as summarized in this chapter, the types of crises that are germane to colleges and universities cut across a broad taxonomy, classified on three dimensions (i.e., domain, responsibility, and declaration), with the impact often distributed across numerous divisions and units.

For individuals interested in the study and practice of crisis leadership in higher education, these findings might seem to suggest that colleges and universities are under siege. Although the challenges are many for college and university leaders, the next chapter attempts to temper this reaction by calling into question the invocation of American higher education in a perpetual state of crisis. Subsequent chapters offer a summary of models, strategies, and concepts to help leaders in higher education move beyond an instrumental, reputation-driven approach to crisis management toward a more dialogic, values-driven approach to crisis leadership as colleges and universities look ahead to the challenges on the horizon.

Reflection Questions for Consideration

1. Scan the current news for the word "crisis." In what ways does the author of the article use this label? Do you agree

with the author's characterization of the event or situation under consideration as a crisis? Why or why not?

2. Using the taxonomy provided in this chapter, map specific crises of significance that have the potential to directly or indirectly impact your unit, department, or institution. How is your institution best prepared or least prepared for each of these potential situations?

3. Which institution-specific crises require the most attention from you or the leaders of your institution (e.g., school shooting, allegations of fraud, student death, campus protests at one particular college or university)? Which broader environmental crises require the most attention from you or the leaders of your institution (e.g., general issues in the higher education environment that present challenges to the larger system, including the crisis in the humanities, the crisis in legal education, the financial crisis in higher education, and the student loan crisis)?

5

Centrality of Communication in the Theory and Practice of Crisis Leadership

With roots in the corporate sector, an examination of crisis management within the context of higher education has garnered increasing attention in recent years, as discussed in chapter 4. Early on, much of the writing on the subject of crisis management (which often includes discussions of risk management, crisis prevention, and, to a certain extent, crisis communication) focused primarily on specific crisis events and episodes, and often provided advice on what immediate actions one might take to minimize dangers and maximize opportunity through the creation and dissemination of public messages. Even in many contemporary texts, the focus is generally on specific strategies and tactics for dealing with events that threaten, disrupt, or endanger an organization, those it serves, or its employees, and on the threats to the reputation of an organization that are triggered by crises (Benoit, 1995, 1997; Coombs, 2015; Heath & Millar, 2004; Mitroff, 2004; Ruff & Aziz, 2003; Sellnow & Seeger, 2013). In many cases, a normative approach is taken based on which practices are found to be most advantageous or detrimental when responding to specific crisis situations, resulting in a series of universal rules or practices. The focus on communication by scholars and practitioners alike has been limited, reflecting a linear view of the role of communication that is both insufficient and incomplete (Ruben & Gigliotti, 2016). For example, when faced with a crisis, it is understood that the organization should offer an immediate response in order to frame the situation before others (i.e., media professionals, competing organizations, influential internal or external stakeholders) adopt an initial frame of their own. Another common crisis management axiom is to offer concise responses in the immediate aftermath of a crisis situation in order to allow more time to learn all of the facts, and perhaps more cynically, to avoid any admission of guilt or wrongdoing that might be used against you in future litigations. A final rule of thumb advanced in the crisis management literature is to avoid the use of "no comment" when responding to crisis-related inquiries. From a public relations perspective, as traditionally conceived, the aim of crisis management, reflected in each of the three previous axioms, is to protect the reputation of individuals and/or an institution, maintain or restore a favorable impression in the eyes of stakeholders, and use communication—which is often conceptualized as message design and dissemination—to shape, influence, and massage public opinion. Recent scholarship in the area of public relations is beginning to move toward a more dialogic model (Bruning, Dials, & Shirka, 2008; Kent, 2013; Kent & Taylor, 2002; Theunissen & Noordin, 2012), which may support the socially constructed and dialogic conceptualization of crisis leadership presented throughout this volume.

Within the context of the crisis management literature, much has been written about the development and implementation of specific strategies for best managing crises, including crisis management plans (Barton, 2001; Coombs, 2006a; Lerbinger, 1997), crisis responses (Benoit, 1995; Coombs, 2006b, 2015; Mitroff, 1994), and post-crisis evaluations (Mitroff, Harrington, & Gai, 1996; Sen & Egelhoff, 1991). The vast literature on these topics acknowledges the importance of crisis preparation, the centrality of clear, quick, and honest communication during all phases of the crisis, and the opportunity for learning following the crisis to inform future crisis responses. Scholars who have taken a communication perspective in their analysis of crisis management tend to emphasize the role, perceptions, and reactions of anticipated and unanticipated audiences; the predetermined goals and direct and indirect messages associated with any official or unofficial announcement during the crisis; and the intended and unintended outcomes associated with a given crisis response. According to Barton (1993), "In a crisis, managers must know their audience. . . . To be effective, your communication during a crisis should have a clearly articulated goal for each audience" (pp. 123, 124). If understood to be "risks that are manifested" (Heath & O'Hair, 2009, p. 10), the ways in which leaders manage, respond to, and evaluate the response to these risks are important topics for communication scholarship. An understanding of process and meaning, both central to the purview of communication scholarship, is critical to an ongoing understanding of the complexity of risk and crisis communication (Heath & O'Hair, 2009).

Managing a crisis, however, is only one part of a leader's responsibility. As Zdziarski, Dunkel, and Rollo (2007) allude to in their writing on the subject:

It is important to distinguish between managing crisis situations and simply responding to them. All too often, crisis management is considered a singular set of actions taken in response to a particular event or incident. Instead, crisis management should be seen as a process that includes a series of stages or phases in which administrators take needed actions. To effectively manage crises, administrators need to take action well before a crisis hits, as well as long after the crisis subsides. A good crisis management system needs to address not only the response phase but the pre- and post-phase as well. (Pp. 46, 47)

Adding to this challenge is the reality that many leadership and social influence outcomes are unplanned, unintentional, unpredicted, and unpredictable, and the consequences are ultimately shaped over time (Gigliotti, Ruben, & Goldthwaite, 2017; Ruben & Gigliotti, 2016). Furthermore, there is no guarantee that the message sent by a leader when attempting to manage a crisis, particularly in the thick of the crisis itself, will be received by those most affected, and in the way the sender intended. Single messages seldom have much impact on broader impressions, and historical context is significant in shaping the design, interpretation, and evolution of messages related to an organizational crisis. For example, when a crisis occurs, it is important to consider the organization's history with crises of a similar type, the leader's past experiences in dealing with crises, and the susceptibilities, expectations, and built-up perceptions of those stakeholders most impacted by the crisis. For these reasons, crisis prevention, crisis management, and crisis communication are only part of the story (Gigliotti & Fortunato, 2017). The focus on crisis leadership, as presented in this chapter, offers a broader framework for understanding what is most at stake during these critical moments in a way that helps to move beyond the commonly held fixation on reputation management.

The Nature of Leadership Communication

Communication, a "universal human experience," is critical to social behavior, yet familiar enough to be taken for granted (Thayer, 1968, 2003). According to Ruben (2005), "Communication is the process through which the social fabric of relationships, groups, organizations, societies, and world order—and disorder—is created and maintained" (p. 294). To be human is to communicate—and, as this chapter explains, to lead is also to communicate. In fact, everything a leader does is communicative in that it sends a message about both the content and the relationship found in any given interaction (Bateson, 1972; Barge, 2014; Watzlawick, Bavelas, & Jackson, 1967).

Leadership, like communication, has become an increasingly popular topic in both scholarly literature and professional training and development (Middlebrooks et al., 2019; Northouse, 2018; Ruben & Gigliotti, 2016). As aptly noted by Fairhurst and Connaughton (2014a), "Leadership is both new and old, a timeless concept that must simultaneously reflect the times yet stay ahead of them. To do so is no small feat, but it is most worthy of pursuit in contemporary organizational life" (p. 24). In many instances, the success or failure of an organization is contingent upon the actions and decisions of its leaders. More than a formal position or responsibility, however, leadership is understood to be a process of social influence that may be accomplished by any organizational actor. This process is shaped by verbal and nonverbal communication and co-constructed between leaders and followers, and by informal as well as formal leaders (Gigliotti et al., 2017; Ruben et al., 2017; Ruben & Gigliotti, 2016). This conceptualization of leadership as a distributed and communicative process is especially relevant for the study of crises in higher education—situations that often demand a collective and collaborative response from multiple units and individuals.

Leadership is a communication endeavor; that is, communication constitutes the DNA of leadership. The inseparability of these two phenomena helps us to analyze the successes and failures of a given leader, for the formal or informal leader with communication competence is often held in high regard by others. It is important to acknowledge that communication competence may involve skills in public speaking and audience analysis, but many nonverbal and material aspects of communication are valuable to effective social influence as well. A leader is often judged not only on what he or she says, but also on the manner in which it is said, the timing and location associated with the communication, the circumstances that preceded this act of verbal communication, and also what may be missing from the leader's remarks. It seems that organizational crises heighten these noted variables associated with leadership communication, making the relationship between crises and leadership communication that much more significant and worthy of our attention (Coombs, 2018; Seeger, 2018).

A communication-oriented way of thinking about leadership allows us to consider the role of communication involved in social influence—which often takes time and relies upon the co-management of meaning with the follower, that is, whoever is receiving the message. Grint (2000) is one of many authors who explore the centrality of communication in the enactment of leadership. In his work on the patterns and actions of leaders, for example, Grint presents an "ensemble of arts" that are organized around communication behaviors. Specifically, he considers "how four particular arts mirror four of the central features of leadership: the invention of an identity, the formulation of a strategic vision, the construction of organizational tactics, and the deployment of persuasive mechanisms to ensure followers actually follow" (p. 27). He classifies these central elements of leadership as philosophical arts (the who), fine arts (the what), martial arts (the how), and performing arts (the why). These carefully calibrated communication responses to organizational and societal problems often shape the legacy of a leader (Grint, 2005).

Also presenting leadership through a communicative lens, Witherspoon (1997) views leadership as "first and foremost a communication process, or set of processes. Every leadership behavior is enacted through communication" (p. 2). In her detailed analysis of discursive leadership, Fairhurst (2007) echoes this idea by illustrating the ways in which leadership is constituted in and through discourse, which can be broadened to include both verbal and nonverbal interactions between leader and follower (Ruben et al., 2017). Consistent with Fairhurst and Connaughton's (2014a) work on the topic, the extant literature on both leadership and communication points to a series of lenses that, "taken collectively, show communication to be central, defining, and constitutive of leadership" (p. 8).

The *Chronicle of Higher Education* and *Inside Higher Ed*, for example, often highlight effective and ineffective leaders in higher education who receive praise or scrutiny for their approach to interpersonal, organizational, and mediated communication. In many ways, the perception of an individual leader hinges upon one's relationships with organizational stakeholders—relationships that are cultivated, sustained, and potentially damaged or deteriorated based on communicative behaviors and decisions. Even though communication is widely recognized as a critical leadership competency for leaders in higher education and beyond, there remains an opportunity for communication thinking to further influence how we understand the dynamics of crisis leadership across colleges and universities. Events that are labeled "crises" provide a backdrop that both highlights and makes complex the role of communication in the ongoing enactment of leadership, and, as discussed in the following section, crisis leadership emerges as a topic worthy of critical exploration.

Deconstructing Crisis Leadership

Distinct from crisis management, the emphasis on crisis leadership allows us to move from a mechanistic or tactical view of the leader's role in crisis to one that is arguably more systematic, proactive, and expansive. Effective crisis leadership goes beyond delivering the most appropriate responses to the most appropriate audiences with the hope that these messages are interpreted as intended by the senders. This simplistic view of communication violates much of what is currently understood about human communication; instead, an understanding of communication theory might lead one to recognize the importance of understanding the organization's history with crisis, appreciating the diverse needs of one's stakeholders, and leading with integrity throughout the entire crisis process (i.e., before, during, and after the critical incident(s)). Crisis leadership involves prevention *and* management, consistency *and* clarity, trust *and* transparency—with communication playing a critical role throughout each phase of any given crisis. As DuBrin (2013) notes, crisis leaders demonstrate charisma, strategic thinking, and an ability to inspire and to express sadness and compassion. By building and maintaining a reservoir of goodwill at the individual and collective levels, a foundation is built for authentic, values-centered dialogue when crises strike, an idea that will be described in more detail in the pages ahead. In his recent writing on the subject of authentic academic leaders, Buller (2018) acknowledges the following, which I have taken the liberty of broadening to also include administrative leaders: "We don't always expect our academic [and administrative] administrators to be embodiments of virtue, but we do expect them to demonstrate integrity and authenticity. So, if we seek to become effective academic [or administrative] leaders, we must strive to become *authentic* academic [or administrative] leaders, to identify the core values that shape our character and decisions, to express to others our commitment to those core values, and then to use those core values as a guide to all of our actions" (pp. 29, 30; emphasis in original). It seems likely that a values-driven reputation and history that serve an individual leader and a collective organization well during times of normalcy are essential for effective leadership and performance during times of crisis, ultimately by providing a solid foundation upon which to stand when the environment seems to be crumbling.

Crisis prevention, management, and communication are not unimportant. Rather, these components are arguably embedded in what is labeled here as crisis leadership. Within higher education, it is increasingly important that academic and administrative leaders learn what is expected by way of crisis prevention and management, while also taking account of the centrality of communication in their leadership behaviors throughout all phases of a given crisis. Recall that from a social construction angle, crises exist when people label them as such, and this labeling of a situation, event, or series of events as a crisis places unique demands on organizational leaders. In his writing on the subject for higher education, Booker (2014) synthesizes the existing literature and posits various leadership competencies that are most essential for each phase of the crisis process. These competencies, which will be discussed further later in the book, include the detection of early warning signs in the environment; the strategic use of communication in preventing, preparing, and containing the crisis; and the promotion of learning throughout the process and at the conclusion of the crisis (p. 19). As a more proactive and holistic approach to dealing with crises in colleges and universities (Mitroff, 2004), the focus on crisis leadership positions us to consider the range of behaviors required at all phases of crisis, ranging from the need for risk assessment tactics that precede a crisis to the learning processes that are rendered meaningful in the aftermath of crisis, all with an eye toward those crises that might be lurking beyond the horizon.

To summarize this section, the practice of crisis leadership involves more than simply conveying the right message(s) to the right audience(s) to uphold the reputation of an institution in the midst of crisis (Gigliotti & Fortunato, 2017). Particularly within our colleges and universities, the act of crisis leadership requires a careful understanding of the types of risks that a unit, department, or institution is currently facing or might one day face and a continual emphasis on learning throughout all phases of the crisis process (Gigliotti & Fortunato, 2017). The reputation-obsessed communication axioms that are so pervasive in the scholarly and professional crisis literature are certainly critical; but so too are the decisions that leaders make in assessing risk, coordinating an assessment of damage(s) done, training and coordinating first responders, and communicating with consistency, clarity, and care in the interest of internal and external audiences. This overemphasis on organizational reputation is fraught with temptations that can lead one to act in a way that privileges the status and perception of the organization over the interests of those individuals who are most likely impacted by any number of risks.

The Role of Communication in the
Social Construction of Crisis

The role of communication in crisis leadership is demonstrated in two models. First, according to Klann (2003), communication, clarity of vision and values, and caring relationships are critical components of crisis leadership. This emphasis on communication and relationships is also central to Muffet-Willett's (2010) research on the topic. In particular, in her crisis leadership practical process model, Muffet-Willett proposes five crisis leadership actions that are most relevant to colleges and universities, with communication and feedback mechanisms situated at various junctures (see figure 5.1). Administrative decision making is critical, but so too are mechanisms for soliciting feedback from key stakeholders across the institution. The model also speaks, indirectly, to the inherent limitations of focusing solely on crisis management or crisis prevention. Crisis leadership encompasses the communication that occurs within senior-level decision making, in organization-wide training initiatives, and in the messages that are sent before, during, and following a crisis.

According to Fairhurst and Sarr (1996), "We become leaders through our ability to decipher and communicate meaning out of complex and confusing situations. . . . There is risk involved when stakes are high" (p. 2). In their analysis of the framing literature, Arnett et al. (2013) advance the following claim: "A leader is not born, but shaped in response to history and through attentiveness to the historical moment. One frames from what is and from an imaginative vision of what might be possible" (p. 72). Approaching this subject from a social construction angle shifts the focus of crisis from phenomena that are "out there" to those that are constituted through communication between leaders

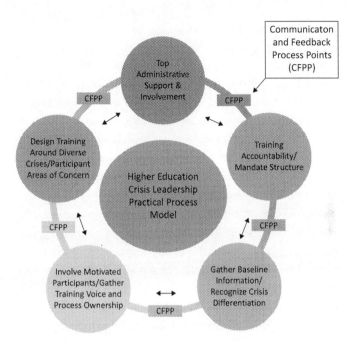

FIG. 5.1. Higher Education Crisis Leadership Practical Process Model (Muffet-Willett, 2010). Reprinted with permission.

and followers. Several claims made by some of the interviewees for this study highlighted the leader's ability to construct and shape the perception of crisis through the act of framing, all the while acknowledging that much lies beyond the individual leader's words and actions. It is through framing that leaders communicatively shape the reality through which others perceive and respond to crisis-like phenomena (Fairhurst, 2010). Grint's (2005) insights on this topic are particularly germane to these findings: "When a crisis occurs the successful leader must become decisive, [and] demonstrate a ruthless ability to focus on the problem and to ignore the siren calls of the sceptics and the cynics. . . . Quite what that crisis might be seems to vary considerably[;] indeed, whether calling a situation 'a crisis' is necessarily the appropriate response seems to depend less on what the situation allegedly 'is' and more on how that situation can be handled most advantageously—or least advantageously—by the leadership" (p. 1468). Put another way, leadership involves the ability to situate and make sense of phenomena in a way that is co-constructed with the individuals who are led. This idea is consistent with Grint's thoughts on the proactive role of leadership in the construction of context: "In effect, leadership involves the social construction of the context that both legitimates a particular form of action and constitutes the world in the process. If that rendering of the context is successful—for there are usually contending and competing renditions—the newly constituted context then limits the alternatives available such that those involved begin to act differently. Or to put it another way, we might begin to consider not what is the *situation*, but how it is *situated*" (pp. 1470, 1471). The pivot from noun to verb takes into consideration the ways in which situations, and crises in particular, are framed and constituted through communication, often to the advantage of the individual involved in the framing.

As discussed in chapter 2, incidents *happen* and crises are *created*. The creation occurs through communication, and it is through communication that crises must be addressed. Furthermore, communication was found to be critical to both the study and practice of crisis leadership, similar to previous studies on the subject of crises and critical incidents in higher education (Agnew, 2014; Garcia, 2015; Gill, 2012; Jacobsen, 2010; Menghini, 2014). For example, as one senior leader stated in an interview:

> The number one theme that has come out of all [live exercises and tabletop simulations] is communication. It's the number one thing that every time needs to be

improved; regardless of how well you think you've done, you think you've prepared, how well you collaborate with others, communication is by far the number one thing that comes out of any of those exercises and any of those live events of things that we can be better [at], can do differently, can do more of. I've never come across a situation where we have learned that we could do less, that we didn't need as much [communication]. (Participant 9)

Given the pervasive interest in communication as it relates to the response to—and ultimately recovery from—crisis situations, what follows is a proposed Crisis Leadership Communication Continuum for scholarly and applied consideration. The continuum builds upon the existing leadership communication literature, reflects the findings from this study, and may be used by individual leaders or departments to encourage more purposeful consideration of the ways in which one might approach communication when faced with a crisis.

A Crisis Leadership Communication Continuum

A crisis leadership framework is useful for academic and administrative leaders in navigating those crises that most specifically occur in institutions of higher education, particularly in understanding the intersections of the core values of an institution, the historical context for the organization, and the types of leadership behaviors that preceded the crisis itself (Gigliotti & Fortunato, 2017). Approaching leadership through the lens of social influence, outcomes are understood to be a consequence of a complex set of factors that include the relationship between leader(s), follower(s), message(s), and context(s) and the interpretive activities of those involved (Ruben & Gigliotti, 2016). Within this process, communication is recognized as an orientation, a standpoint, a way of understanding leadership dynamics that extends beyond the study of discourse. Bearing this in mind, the continuum described here addresses the content of a leader's response during crisis situations; but it also considers the leader's relationships with followers, one's understanding of organizational history, and one's recognition of the precedent-setting nature of leadership communication. This perspective allows leaders to consider crisis leadership communication as more than the public crisis response. Crisis leadership involves, but extends beyond, reputation management, and it is the result of an ongoing series of interactions with organizational stakeholders.

These findings, coupled with the growing body of scholarship on leadership communication, crisis communication, and crisis leadership, led to development of a Crisis Leadership Communication Continuum. As depicted in figure 5.2, the continuum ranges from compliance to dialogue, with self-focus and other-focus positioned on opposite ends of the continuum. The model is meant to illustrate two opposing tensions that leaders must negotiate when communicating with internal and external audiences. Presented as a continuum, the framework suggests that individuals might be oriented more toward one direction than another within the continuum. For example, when crisis situations impact colleges and universities, the reaction often is a "measured, legalistic response that so often dominates crisis management in academe" (Stripling & Thomason, 2015, para. 2), what is characterized here as a "compliance" approach in the model. This tendency to engage in self-oriented, compliance-driven communication in response to crisis situations is pervasive in higher education, as in many other sectors, and one might argue that concern for the reputation of the institution is the primary factor driving communication decisions.

Consider, for example, the type of communication that often takes place during press conferences following an active shooter situation, of which we have far too many to reflect upon. The tendency is for leaders to report primarily on the facts of the event while carefully avoiding any acknowledgment of guilt or wrongdoing. On the opposite end of the continuum lies the tension of an other-oriented, dialogue-driven response—one that is arguably motivated by a primary concern for those stakeholders most affected by the crisis. Within this orientation, leaders are guided by a desire to recognize, learn from, and appropriately address the needs, expectations, values, and concerns of institutional stakeholders and invite them to co-construct the path forward for the institution. This latter approach privileges the role of communication as more than a tool for leadership influence. Instead, it allows for the conceptual and operational switch from a public relations/reputation-centered understanding of crisis leadership to a dialogic, follower-centered approach that best meets the multiple demands and concerns of stakeholders. Note that this model does not dismiss the need for a measured, legalistic response to campus emergencies. Referring to the earlier example of the post-shooting press conference, leaders must certainly acknowledge the legal counsel provided during situations of this kind, while also demonstrating a genuine concern for the victims of the incident and a sincere desire to learn from the situation. In such cases, one might argue that the reaction from stakeholders would be less favorable if the compliance-oriented response were the only type of communication to occur before, during, or following a crisis. Furthermore, a restricted compliance- and reputation-oriented response to campus crisis limits the potential for institutional learning and growth that might otherwise be possible.

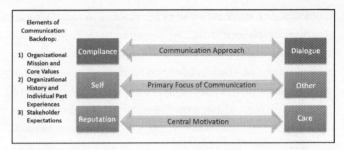

FIG. 5.2. Crisis Leadership Communication Continuum.

A broader communication backdrop situates any crisis leadership interactions. This backdrop influences leadership decision-making and communication behaviors, and it contributes to the way individuals might perceive leadership actions. The backdrop consists of the mission and core values of the organization, past experiences with crisis situations, and stakeholder expectations—all of which ultimately shape the ways in which leaders communicate in times of crisis. Finally, given that leadership communication actually begins prior to the crisis itself, it is important to acknowledge that there is an ongoing history that precedes crisis situations, and the crisis shines the spotlight on leadership behaviors that might not otherwise receive immediate or focused attention.

This framework acknowledges the utility of approaching crisis leadership through a values-centered lens—an orientation that positions clarity, consistency, and congruency between the way that one leads during any given crisis and those core values that are most critical to an institution. For example, in 1982, when several Tylenol Extra-Strength capsules were replaced with cyanide-laced capsules, which led to the death of seven people, Johnson & Johnson, which produces Tylenol, was forced to immediately respond to a situation that threatened the health and safety of its "patients" —a stakeholder group recognized as the priority in their "Credo" (Johnson & Johnson, 2019). At the same time, the decisions made by organizational leaders would also have a lasting impact on the perception of the company by a wide array of current *and* future stakeholders. As Adubato (2009) posits, "Although it occurred in a very different media environment than our present one, this case is still a valuable example of how a company should communicate when its reputation, as well as its financial survival, is on the line" (p. 12). Crises often test the core values of an organization, and by using their credo as a guide for decision making and communication in recalling the Tylenol product from every provider, Johnson & Johnson was successful in both protecting its reputation and demonstrating a genuine commitment to the care of its patients.

The University of Oklahoma, an institution that prides itself on the vision of achieving "national and international recognition for excellence as a pacesetter institution in its commitment to building and maintaining a diverse and inclusive community," provides another relevant example of this type of response (University of Oklahoma, 2018). This noble mission and the underlying values associated with this charge were called into question on March 9, 2015, when several brothers from Sigma Alpha Epsilon (SAE) fraternity were caught on video singing a racist anthem. Immediately following the incident, SAE national headquarters shut down the chapter, and the members were given two days to vacate the university-owned property (Ohlheiser, 2015). Former president David Boren received praise for his prompt and bold response to the crisis, a response that also carried some inherent legal risks (Stripling & Thomason, 2015). Boren called the students "disgraceful" and expelled them "because of [their] leadership role in leading a racist and exclusionary chant which has created a hostile educational environment for others." His swift public response appeared to be driven by the values upheld and promoted by the institution, along with perhaps Boren's own personal core values (Buller, 2018). In response to SAE members finding a place to live, Boren publicly declared that "we do not provide student services for racists and bigots." According to Bolman and Gallos (2011), "Whether academic leaders realize it or not, they always have choices about how to frame and interpret their world—and their choices are fateful" (p. 22).[1]

Both the Johnson & Johnson example and the remarks by President Boren also illustrate the limitations of a dichotomous way of thinking about crisis communication, and the model does not attempt to prescribe the ways in which one should communicate when faced with crisis. As illustrated by the triangular fulcrums in the center of each dimension of the model, leaders must find the right balance in navigating the tensions associated with crisis communication while remaining sensitive to the three pervasive factors that play an active role in the backdrop. As a reflective tool, individuals and organizations may choose to map previous public statements to this model in order to discuss some of the perceived strengths of this approach, along with any limitations attributed to this type of response, with the goal of encouraging greater reflexivity and intentionality as it relates to how one approaches communication when faced with an organizational crisis.

Conclusion

In his summary of the annual American Marketing Association higher education conference, Lee Gardner (2016) from the *Chronicle of Higher Education* described the emphasis by attendees on aligning public statements with the institution's missions and values with the desire for "subsequent actions [to] validate their words" during moments of crisis. As Rebecca John, vice president for marketing and communication at Augsburg College, noted at the conference, "We are now in a post–'thoughts-and-prayers' world and an insincere or ineffective response may be worse than no response at all." These insights reflect various comments noted by senior administrators with whom I spoke. As one senior respondent posited:

> I think at the end of the day, I think honesty works best and the only kind of leader that I ever want to work for is someone who will do what is right and then figure out the narrative after. If you ever make decisions based on what the narrative will look like, I think you're doing it wrong. That becomes a spin game. I just think if we try to make it *look like* we're doing the right thing as opposed to doing the right thing, people are smart enough to read through that. That can be really tough, but I really think that needs to be the most singular value that any leader that I would want to work for would have. (Participant 1; emphasis added)

This sentiment was shared by many of the participants of this study. A review of the competencies, skills, and values identified as most critical for crisis leadership in higher education, which are discussed in more detail in the following chapter, reflects the desire for a more authentic, honest, and stakeholder-centered communication strategy that is built around integrity, principles, and "doing what is right" (Participant 16). As another leader described his institution's approach to crisis leadership, "The administration naturally wants to protect [their] brand and protect the university's reputation which has taken years to build up and, you know, which it's earned, which is legitimate and that's a legitimate concern, but service to the brand can't take precedence over service to the truth or doing things right or acting according to your mission statement" (Participant 8). Reflecting on the nature of dialogue, Arnett and Arneson's (1999) summary of Buber holds true: "Life is lived in the *between*—between persons, between person and event, between person and idea, even in crisis. Life is not captured in the other or in me, but between us" (p. 128).

Many of the leaders whom I interviewed identified the potential issues with approaching crisis communication in higher education from a self-focused, compliance-oriented, and reputation-driven position—one that is increasingly common. According to one senior leader, "I think our greatest shortcoming sometimes is that we focus too much on reputational risk. I think you will find that across the board in higher education. . . . Focusing on reputational risk over students, over people, is a huge shortcoming" (Participant 13). She went on to acknowledge one of the provocative lessons found in *The Hunting Ground*, a popular documentary film about rape crimes on college and university campuses across the country: "In a crisis situation, nobody is going to follow somebody who's reading a script and saying now we're supposed to do this. Watch *The Hunting Ground*. It will give you a nugget of wow, that institutional reputation, that overly scripted talking point. We just hammer on the same message no matter how ridiculous it is. It's off-putting" (Participant 13). Recognizing the limitations of a linear, transactional approach to leadership communication, the message alone is not sufficient. As another senior leader, one with University Communications responsibilities, acknowledged: "The easiest way to handle a crisis is to say, 'This is a problem. This is what we're going to do. This is when we're going to do it,' and then do it. If you do those three things, you can communicate not as well and come out the other end quite in good health. If you don't do those things, well then you can communicate as well as you want, you probably won't get very far" (Participant 20). Consider again the Crisis Leadership Communication Continuum in figure 5.2. It is possible to envision a number of factors that may uphold, influence, and shape stakeholder perceptions of leadership communication, including past precedent, leadership actions and behaviors, and the duration and degree of severity associated with the present crisis. As one respondent commented, the pervasive emphasis on reputation "clouds" leadership communication, and "time is not on our side. As leaders, time is way against leadership. Time is way against thoughtful leadership, thoughtful, value-driven leadership. It's just against it, because thoughtfulness can't be rushed. Yet that is the expectation today in crises" (Participant 34). A nuanced understanding of communication theory helps to point out the inherent limitations of a public relations or reputation-oriented approach to crisis leadership, particularly in juxtaposing it with what one senior leader labeled a genuine approach, or what could also be characterized as a dialogic approach. As he offered, "The genuine part is to really understand what's going on and to understand it from the lens of the people involved, which means you have to suspend your own lens. The goal is simply to understand" (Participant 35). The human side of academic and administrative leadership is made especially prominent when dealing with crises of significance.

Finally, it is worth reiterating that this continuum is not meant to be a formulaic recipe for message design and delivery. Rather, the goal of the framework is to encourage greater reflection on behalf of leaders when considering the ways that they communicate and the content of their messages as well as greater attention to the multiple needs of multiple stakeholders and to the values that are important to the institution. As a conceptual framework designed to invite greater complexity and nuance to contemporary thinking around issues of crisis leadership and communication, this continuum can help to assess the type of communication leaders engage in during crisis situations, and it may also serve as a cautionary reminder for leaders of the limitations inherent in approaching the response to crisis situations from a purely public relations or reputation-oriented lens. Finally, in light of the social construction approach taken throughout this text, the continuum seeks to address the many variables involved in the construction process, including leaders, stakeholders, message infrastructure, media environment, and historical context, all the while bringing attention to the nonverbal and material aspects of communication that shape leader-follower interactions. The complexity of crisis leadership in higher education comes through clearly in this chapter, and as discussed in the following chapter, part of this complexity involves the wide array of competencies, skills, and values expected of leaders when dealing with organizational and environmental crises—several of which are embedded in this continuum.

Reflection Questions for Consideration

1. Which of the communication concepts offered in this chapter do you find to be the most useful for the study and practice of crisis leadership in higher education?
2. How would you distinguish crisis prevention and crisis management from crisis leadership? What do you see as some of the more valuable principles of crisis leadership based on the summary presented in this chapter?

3. Using the Crisis Leadership Communication Continuum (figure 5.2) as a guide, review examples of public responses to crises at your institution or another institution. Where would you position these responses on this continuum? Which aspects of the responses do you find most or least effective, and in what ways is the effectiveness of the response associated with the criteria detailed in the continuum?

6

Crisis Adaptation of Leadership Competencies Scorecard for Leaders in Higher Education

As distinct from crisis management, crisis leadership, particularly within higher education, involves and extends beyond risk assessment, crisis prevention, and reputation management. There is a more expansive collection of needed competencies, skills, and values associated with leadership during crisis situations that is much broader than many of the public relations–driven dimensions that currently appear in many crisis-oriented books, manuals, and scholarly articles. The tendency to foreground and privilege the protection of an organization's reputation over the many other requisite crisis leadership behaviors is not only limited, but it may also be detrimental to one's overall leadership effectiveness. As one senior administrator suggested, the propensity to approach crisis leadership through a reputation-centered focus can lead administrators to consider "not what is the right thing to do, but what impact is this going to have" (Participant 34). This chapter details a broad portfolio of competencies required for leadership during these critical, public, and high-stakes moments of organizational disruption based on my interview data, and the chapter concludes with two distinct higher education vignettes—one in which many of the competencies are apparent, and another that illustrates a clear void.

An Introduction to the Competency Model: Vertical and Horizontal Leadership Needs

When asked to describe the competencies, skills, or values they found to be most useful to their roles as senior leaders during times of perceived crisis, the senior leaders offered numerous responses. Ruben's (2012) leadership competencies scorecard provides a useful heuristic for thinking through the various characteristics of effective crisis leadership. Although the scorecard was not designed to focus exclusively on crisis situations, nor was the scorecard used by the researcher as a primary theoretical construct for this project, the findings from this project map directly to the scorecard in a way that may be valuable for individuals and teams who seek to identify and further develop their capacity in these areas. The leadership competencies scorecard is the result of Ruben's synthesis of the extensive professional literature on leadership that led to the development of a diverse portfolio of requisite competencies organized around five broad areas: analytic competencies, personal competencies, communication competencies, organizational competencies, and positional competencies. Each of these broad competency areas encompasses a number of themes, as illustrated in table 6.1. In his description of these competency themes, Ruben indicates that many of the challenges that leaders face require a diverse portfolio of knowledge and skills, and the ability to analyze situations and employ any number of competencies.

For any formal leadership role, there exists a need for position-, institution-, and sector-specific or "vertical"

TABLE 6.1 Leadership Competency Scorecard 2.0:
Five Major Competency Themes, Each Including a
Number of Specific Competency Areas

ANALYTIC	PERSONAL	ORGANIZATIONAL	POSITIONAL	COMMUNICATION
Self-Assessment	Character, Personal Values, & Ethics	Vision-Setting, Strategy Development, Goal-Setting	Education	Credibility & Trust
Problem-Definition	Cognitive Ability & Creativity	Management & Supervision	Experience	Influence & Persuasion
Stakeholder Analysis	Enthusiasm	Information/ Knowledge Management and Boundary Spanning	Expertise	Interpersonal and Group Relations, and Team Building
Systems/ Organizational Analysis	High-Standards	Technological Capability	Knowledge of Sector	Listening, Attention, Questioning, & Learning
Analysis of Technology to Support Leadership	Personal Conviction & Persistence	Collaborative Decision Making and Empowerment	Knowledge of Organization	Writing and Public Speaking
Problem-Solving	Self-Discipline & Self-Confidence	Teaching & Coaching	Familiarity with Work	Diversity and Intercultural Relations
Review & Analysis of Results	Role Modeling	Change, Risk and Crisis Management	Professional Involvement	Facilitation, Negotiation, and Conflict Resolution

Source: Ruben (2012).

competencies and crosscutting or "horizontal" competencies, as illustrated in figure 6.1 (Gigliotti, 2019; Ruben, 2012; Ruben et al., 2017). When crises impact a college or university, the need arises for a leader to navigate the unique requirements of a given position, role, and institution. This vertical expertise in a particular function of the university is important in helping the leader understand the specific nature of a given crisis and the capabilities and deficiencies of the institution. For example, familiarity with Title IX proves useful in navigating campus sexual assaults, and experience with an institution's computer security infrastructure is critical when dealing with an attempted cyberattack. Another area where vertical expertise is useful involves a leader's understanding of the unique protocols, policies, norms, and expectations based on the institutional type. Despite their many similarities, important differences exist across religiously affiliated universities, large public institutions, community colleges, and for-profit universities. An understanding of these cultural and structural differences is critical as leaders attempt to navigate the vertical demands associated with leading their institutions. Additionally, the responsibilities during crisis situations vary based on one's role in the institution. Existing protocols will likely differentiate the anticipated expectations based on individual roles. If a decision is made to evacuate the campus, for example, who makes the final determination, who communicates the decision to the university community, who coordinates with any local, state, or national officials, and which personnel are deemed essential during the evacuation period? If faced with an active shooter, in what ways are security decisions made, communicated, and implemented based on one's institutional role? The knowledge and skill required for the role—the requisite competencies—are in many ways tailored around the structure, culture, and organizational history of a specific institution, along with the experience and expertise that one brings based on one's work in a specific functional area.

Despite the unique needs of an institution and the unique expectations for colleges and universities, numerous crosscutting or "horizontal" competencies exist (Gigliotti, 2019;

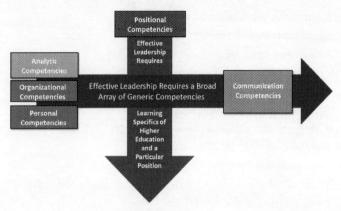

FIG. 6.1. Two-Dimensional Leadership Competencies Model (Ruben, 2012; Ruben, De Lisi, & Gigliotti, 2017).

Ruben, 2012; Ruben et al., 2017) that are generally expected of leaders across colleges and universities, and even across institutions of higher education and other industries and sectors. Figure 6.1 presents the knowledge and skill required of leaders to cut across an array of analytic, organizational, personal, and communication domains. Both sets of competencies—vertical and horizontal—are critical to effective leadership during times of normalcy, and the demands become increasingly heightened during crises. The competencies, skills, and values associated with crisis leadership presented in this chapter align directly with these five competency areas, with communication being arguably the most critical competency area for the practice of crisis leadership in higher education.

Prominent Competencies for Effective Crisis Leadership

The following competencies were each recognized by more than one senior administrator as essential for effective crisis leadership in higher education:

- analysis, synthesis, and triage
- adaptability/flexibility
- calmness
- care and aftercare
- collaboration
- confidence and courage
- empathy and compassion
- humility
- institutional focus
- information gathering and dissemination
- learning
- presence and availability
- resilience
- safety
- transparency and honesty
- trust

In addition to these competencies, appropriate preparation was identified as critical for leadership effectiveness in crisis situations, along with the ability to define crisis, detect and monitor crisis, and analyze stakeholder perceptions. Using Ruben's scorecard as a conceptual guide and the findings from this project as empirical evidence, table 6.2 provides a crisis adaptation of the scorecard that can be used to analyze the leadership behaviors demonstrated in crisis case studies, to guide leaders during periods of crisis, and to prepare future leaders in formal and informal training and development programs.

The presentation and organization of these critical competencies listed in table 6.2 are not meant to be exhaustive; rather, they reflect the prominent characteristics that emerged from my conversations with college and university leaders. The competency framework helps us to see the ways in which leadership is manifested across distinct competency themes (i.e., analytical, personal, organizational, positional, and

TABLE 6.2. Crisis Adaptation of Leadership Competencies Scorecard

ANALYTIC COMPETENCIES	PERSONAL COMPETENCIES	ORGANIZATIONAL COMPETENCIES	POSITIONAL COMPETENCIES	COMMUNICATION COMPETENCIES
An ability to analyze the situation, the environment, and the perceptions from diverse stakeholders, including the following:	An array of personal values associated with the practice of crisis leadership, including:	An understanding of the policies, behaviors, and norms that require organizational abilities and focus on the organization as a unit of analysis:	An understanding of the positional and sector-specific roles, responsibilities, and expectations, based on Ruben's (2012) original positional themes:	An understanding of communication and the ability to effectively communicate before, during, and following crisis, based on Ruben's (2012) original communication themes:
• analysis, synthesis, and triage	• calmness	• adaptable/flexible	• education	• credibility and trust
• defining crisis	• care and aftercare	• familiarity with crisis management plans, procedures, and protocols	• experience	• influence and persuasion
• detecting and monitoring crisis	• collaboration	• information and knowledge management	• expertise	• interpersonal and group relations, and team building
• analyzing stakeholder perceptions	• confidence and courage	• institutional focus	• knowledge of sector	• listening, attention, questioning, and learning
	• empathy and compassion	• learning	• knowledge of discipline	• writing and public speaking
	• humility	• safety	• knowledge of organization	• diversity and intercultural relations
	• presence and availability		• familiarity with work	• facilitation, negotiation, and conflict resolution
	• resilience		• professional involvement	
	• transparency and honesty		• knowledge of crisis avoidance, prevention, and resolution within one's discipline/ department and within higher education more broadly	
	• trust			

communication competencies) and subcompetencies, particularly those areas that reflect the variety of popular leadership theories and models that Ruben examined in his original synthesis. Additionally, through the two-dimensional illustration and language offered in this chapter, the model makes clear that many crisis leadership competencies are reflective of position, experience, and institution, and others are very much crosscutting in nature. Thus, for aspiring and current leaders in higher education, the model indicates the need to scan one's institutional context, the higher education context, and the broader environment for lessons on crisis leadership. Certainly, higher education is unique, but not so unique as to disregard the learning that can—and should—happen across sectors.

Ways of Using the Scorecard for Crisis Leadership Development

The scorecard, along with the guiding questions below, may be of use for formal, informal, and aspiring leaders in higher education and for individuals with coaching functions (e.g., formal coach, manager, leadership educator) who are interested in using the tool as a mechanism for preparing faculty, staff, and students for crisis leadership in higher education. Similar to the approach offered in Ruben's (2012) original scorecard, you might consider ranking yourself on a scale of 1 to 5 as it relates to your *understanding* of the broader competency theme and subcompetencies within each domain presented in table 6.2, along with your *skill* in each of these areas. The following questions, which have been adapted from Ruben (2006) and Gigliotti (2019), may be used as a guide for individuals who assess both their knowledge and skill with the various competency themes and subcompetencies provided in table 6.2.

- In which of the crisis leadership competency areas do you have the highest level of *understanding*?
- In which of the crisis leadership competency areas do you have the highest level of *skill*?
- What did you learn about yourself after ranking your understanding and skill for each of these competencies?
- Was there anything that surprised you as you reviewed the results to this self-assessment?
- As you reflect on your experience dealing with crisis situations, which of the leadership competency areas has most likely contributed to your success?
- In which of the crisis leadership competency areas would you most like to improve your *understanding*? Are there specific subcompetency areas where you believe improvement would be particularly beneficial? What specific actions might you take to further develop your understanding of this competency and/or subcompetency?
- In which of the crisis leadership competency areas would you most like to improve your *skill*? Are there specific subcompetency areas where you believe improvement would be particularly beneficial? What specific actions might you take to further develop your ability to practice this competency and/or subcompetency?
- What competency and subcompetency areas have the greatest gap and/or smallest gap between your understanding and your skill level? In what ways does this large gap and/or small gap present challenges or assist in your ability to lead during crisis situations?
- As you think about the unit, organization, and/or sector within which you work, which of the crisis leadership competencies is most likely preferred in formal leaders? In informal leaders? Do your knowledge and/or skills in this preferred competency contribute to your ability to lead in this specific unit, organization, and/or sector?

- Review the array of subcompetencies within the competency framework. Which of these subcompetencies do you believe is most critical for effective crisis leadership? Why?
- In what ways do the findings of this assessment map onto the results of any other leadership or personality assessment that you have completed in the past (e.g., Clifton-Strengths, DISC, Myers-Briggs, True Colors)?
- Ask a trusted colleague, family member, or friend to complete the scorecard based on their perceptions of your knowledge and skills. Review the results of their assessment of you and compare the findings with those from your self-assessment.
  - In what ways do the findings overlap? What do you think contributes to the similar results?
  - In what ways do the findings differ from one another? What do you think contributes to the different results?
  - How do the results from the assessment by a family member or friend compare or contrast with those of a professional colleague or co-worker? For what reasons might the perceptions of you be similar or different based on their role and their relationship with you?

These questions offer various ways to think about crisis leadership competencies, and one might add other competencies required in times of crisis. Both one's self-perception and the perception of others that these questions seek to probe can also be useful for training and development efforts designed for formal, informal, and aspiring leaders in higher education.

Values-Centered Academic Leadership

At their core, crises are disorienting, destabilizing, and disruptive. In addition to the competencies noted above, leaders with whom I spoke for this project routinely noted the importance of "doing the right thing" and "values-based leadership" in our discussions of crisis leadership, and it is these core principles that provide direction, guidance, and stability when all else seems to fail. As described in the previous chapter, Buller (2018) argues in support of a values-based approach to college administration, a sentiment that I have come to appreciate and endorse based on my own experiences and research. As he posits: "We don't always expect our academic leaders to be embodiments of virtue, but we do expect them to demonstrate integrity and authenticity. So, if we seek to become effective academic leaders, we must strive to become *authentic* academic leaders, to identify the core values that shape our character and decisions, to express to others our commitment to those core values, and then to use those core values as a guide to all our actions" (pp. 29, 30). These core values, as summarized by Buller, "are certainly not [academic leaders'] *only* values; they're merely the principles that tend to take precedence over other principles when there is a conflict" (p. 24). The core values of an academic leader, illustrated in figure 6.2, are significantly informed and shaped by a number of external factors that influence leadership behaviors.

Buller goes on to distinguish three sources of motivation for leaders of all kinds:

- Product-oriented motivation occurs when a leader is attracted by the desire to achieve a specific goal.
- Process-oriented motivation occurs when a leader's focus is directed more toward the activity that will produce a goal than the goal itself.
- Principle-oriented motivation occurs when a leader's values inspire the leader to act in a certain way regardless of product (goal) or process (the system in which he or she operates). (P. 155)

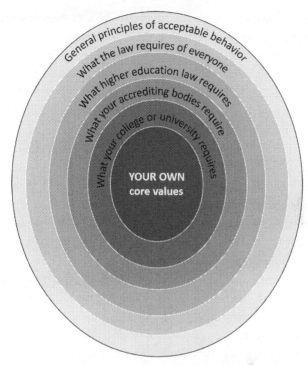

FIG. 6.2. The Core Values of an Academic Leader (Buller, 2018). Reprinted with permission.

Organizational crises, or what Buller refers to as "scandals," are often the result of an overemphasis on product or process over principles. The discovery of eighteen years of academic fraud involving athletes at the University of North Carolina at Chapel Hill, the misreporting of data by the Temple University Fox School of Business to *U.S. News and World Report*, and the alleged cover-up of sexual harassment complaints at the University of Southern California may be perceived to be examples of a motivation for product or process over principle by leaders of the respective institution.

Each of these examples of crises of product or process over principles can be juxtaposed with a host of examples that seem to demonstrate values in action across colleges and universities. For example, in response to growing campus unrest across the country, including a violent protest by "150 masked agitators" at the University of California, Berkeley leading up to a scheduled talk by Breitbart editor and right-wing commentator Milo Yiannopoulous, the University of California developed the National Center for Free Speech and Civic Engagement. According to UC president Janet Napolitano, "Our country needs an outlet to grapple with changing views on the First Amendment and what these mean for America and how our democracy functions." In their online description of the center, the connection to the free speech movement's origin at Berkeley is made clear, with a goal of "[restoring] trust in the value and importance of free speech among college students, other members of university communities, and broader society" (National Center for Free Speech and Civic Engagement, 2019).

Another example of a values-driven approach takes us to the Citadel, a military college in South Carolina, which had to respond quickly to a situation that unfortunately mirrors to some degree what has been occurring on other college and university campuses: photographs of "a group of student cadets [singing] Christmas carols while wearing pointy white pillowcases with eyeholes on their heads, evoking the Ku Klux Klan" (Lederman, 2018). Lederman goes on to summarize the Citadel's approach to responding to the crisis—an ongoing response that emphasized transparency, core values, and frequent practice—which was the focus of a presentation at the annual meeting of the National Association of College and University Business Officers: "Citadel officials worked through case studies on a regular basis . . . to try to build muscle memory and anticipate scenarios so they were as prepared as possible for the real thing. Part of every exercise involved asking what the likeliest scenarios were, as well as the 'most dangerous' possible outcomes. That served them well when local reporters called and said the newspaper planned to publish news of the photographs of the cadets in apparent Klan attire—and told Citadel officials they had 10 minutes to provide a statement." Their public statement did come out within the imposed deadline, acknowledging that "the photographs were 'not consistent with our core values of honor, duty, and respect'" and that the college "had begun suspension proceedings against the involved cadets." The behaviors of the cadets cut at the core of honor, duty, and respect, and the bold, prompt, and clear response by the senior leaders of the institution—a result of careful rehearsal, preparation, and coordination—appeared to serve the institution well during this unsettling moment.

Conclusion

The examples of values-driven and values-absent responses to crises in higher education are plentiful, and any attempt to fully detail the crises within these pages would be incomplete and potentially limited. The brief vignettes of crises in this chapter and throughout the book offer windows into crises of relevance facing college and universities. These situations require a blend of both "vertical" and "horizontal" competencies, along with an understanding of and sincere commitment to the core values that guide both the individual and the organization. In my ongoing review of declared "crises" detailed in higher education news outlets, the pattern is becoming increasingly clear and predictable—articulating the importance of one's core values is critical, but not sufficient. Rather, the actions to follow a crisis, coupled with the ways in which senior leaders directly and indirectly engage and interact with affected stakeholders, can be interpreted as manifestations of values in practice. As Buller (2018) concludes in his book, "The essence of authentic leadership . . . is knowing who you are as a person, particularly with regard to your values, perspectives, personal opinions, and the system you use to apply all of these to your work and life" (p. 171). These values take center stage when crises strike, and the multiple audiences will be waiting to observe the performance that follows during these defining moments.

Reflection Questions for Consideration

1. Of the dominant competencies, skills, and guiding values for effective crisis leadership noted in this chapter, which do you believe are your primary areas of strength? Which areas would you hope to develop further?

2. Identify a leader in higher education who led admirably during a crisis situation. In which of the competency themes are they most knowledgeable and/or skilled, and in what ways has their mastery of this competency contributed to their ability to lead effectively in moments of crisis?

3. Compare and contrast a crisis response where core values were made prominent with one that seemed to be focused solely on protecting the reputation of the unit, department, or institution. Why is there a tendency to privilege reputation protection over core values during periods of institutional crisis, and in what ways can the emphasis on values ultimately lead to an enhanced reputation?

7

Implications for Effective Crisis Leadership in Higher Education

Many pundits and stakeholders proclaim—often with great confidence and conviction—the unfolding "crisis in higher education." For example, in her book *American Higher Education in Crisis? What Everyone Needs to Know*, Blumenstyk (2014) posits the following in her introduction: "The doomsday narrative is seemingly everywhere, with predictions of a massive 'shake-out' coming to the postsecondary-education landscape because of rising costs and recession-weakened finances, and of a 'college bubble' on the verge of bursting under the crushing weight of student debt" (p. 2). This idea echoes concerns by Readings (1996) of the "university in ruins," due in part to an external legitimation crisis whereby "it is no longer clear what the place of the University is within society nor what the exact nature of that society is" (p. 2).

There exists a plethora of examples of recent crises to befall institutions of higher education in the United States. In some cases, these crisis situations are the direct result of inadequate planning or preparation on behalf of the leaders of the institution. In other examples, the source of the crisis is much more complex, unpredictable, and multifaceted. Weighing heavily on many senior leaders in higher education is a wide array of challenges, including the erosion of public trust (Fingerhut, 2017), growing scrutiny from a wide range of internal and external stakeholders (Ruben et al., 2017), a concerning and uncertain financial outlook (Calderon & Jones, 2017), and ongoing issues related to access, affordability, and adequate job preparation. The combination of high-profile crises at well-known colleges and universities, many of which are highlighted throughout this book, with the ongoing critiques leveled at colleges and universities for being "out of touch," "too expensive," and, to some (including 58 percent of Republicans and Republican-leaning independents, based on a 2017 Pew survey), "harmful," creates a backdrop against which higher education becomes the subject of widespread criticism. For some, a clear argument can be made about the perpetual state of "crisis" facing the entire sector of American higher education—a sentiment that is reinforced with each new scandal or school closure announcement. The view of crisis put forth in this book—that it is socially constructed, often subjective, and communication-driven—invites us to treat crisis as less of a given, or, as Roitman (2014) argues, to "put less faith in crisis" (p. 13), and to consider the relative conditions of crisis based on the perceptions of diverse stakeholders.

A Sector "in Crisis"?

An analysis of the media's attempt to exaggerate crises in higher education lies beyond the scope of this project due to decisions regarding research design; however, the initial evidence seems to suggest that, although the discourse of crisis in higher education is certainly provocative, it may be unfair to depict the sector as being in a perpetual state of crisis. As a senior leader representing Academic Affairs offered: "I think [the description of higher education in crisis] is overblown. I do. I think what we are facing is somewhat of a public perception problem. I don't think we get our message out very well about what we're all about. Therefore, the public draws their own conclusions" (Participant 29). Others challenged the public impression that "the sky is falling" (Participant 14), and as one leader suggested, "I'm not trying to diminish the word 'crisis,' but I do think it could be indeed overblown because it's a provocative statement and makes people read the *Chronicle* [*of Higher Education*]" (Participant 3). Rather than pursue leadership in higher education as if an entire sector is in crisis, it may be more helpful for leaders to routinely consider "to whom" higher education is in crisis as they navigate the array of challenges that colleges and universities now face. These challenges are significant and show no signs of decline. A review of higher education–related news coverage, coupled with my conversations with senior leaders for this project, presents a sector in flux as leaders grapple with a wide array of major issues— issues that could certainly elevate to the level of crisis— including, but not limited to, financial pressures, campus violence and threats to student safety, recurring debates surrounding issues of academic freedom and free speech, and campus unrest triggered by ongoing racial tensions. There are very clear examples of individual institutions dealing with financial issues that threaten their long-term survival, coupled with others who currently face isolated crisis-like situations, such as those detailed in the preceding chapter. The child abuse scandal at Penn State and the gymnast abuse scandal at Michigan State, in addition to the devastating impact of Hurricane Katrina at Loyola University and Hurricane Maria at the University of Puerto Rico, for example, are very clear examples of organizational crises. However, it appears that many of the general issues colleges and universities must address are better understood as challenges that demand leadership attention, with the designation of "crisis" reserved for those isolated events or situations of significant magnitude that threaten reputations, impact the lives of those involved in the institution, disrupt the ways in which the organization functions, have a cascading influence on leadership responsibilities and obligations across units/divisions, and require an immediate response from leaders.

In her work on the subject, Roitman (2014) claims that "crisis is an omnipresent sign in almost all forms of narrative today; it is mobilized as the defining category of historical situations, past and present" (p. 3). The ubiquitous and casual invocation of crisis cuts across organizational sectors and bodies of literature; and as illustrated in the findings from the content analysis for this project, the popularity of crisis holds true for institutions of higher education. As suggested by risk and crisis communication scholar Matthew Seeger, "crisis is a growth industry" (personal communication, March 13, 2018), and crisis becomes a useful construct through which to bracket, punctuate, and make sense of events or situations with which we must contend. An interrogation of the ways in which crises are shaped through communication, however, allows us to problematize the very use of the word "crisis" as a descriptor or point of reference, such as that supported by Roitman (2014) in this extended passage:

> Ultimately, I invite the reader to put less faith in crisis, which means asking what is at stake with crisis in-and-of-itself. "Crisis" is a term that is bound up in the predicament of signifying human history, often serving as a transcendental placeholder in ostensible solutions to that problem. In that sense, the term "crisis" serves as a primary enabling blind spot for the production of knowledge. That is, crisis is a point of view, or an observation, which itself is not

viewed or observed. I apprehend the concept of crisis through the metaphor of a blind spot so as to apprehend crisis as an observation that, like all observations or cognitions, does not account for the very conditions of its observation. Consequentially, making that blind spot visible means asking questions about how we produce significance for ourselves. (P. 13)

Certain narratives and questions remain possible through the invocation of crisis, yet this very invocation simultaneously forecloses other possibilities, an idea that echoes what some have referred to as the "trivialization of crisis" (Arnett, 2006; Lasch, 1991; Persuit, 2013). Rather than take the notion of crisis for granted, this focus on how we bring attention to, create, or manufacture crisis aligns with the scope and findings of this exploration into crisis in higher education whereby crisis is both questioned and problematized as a topic for scholarly inquiry and an area of focus for leaders in higher education.

The leaders I interviewed represent institutions that recently dealt with a relatively high-profile event associated with one of the crisis types identified in chapter 4 (e.g., academic crisis, athletics crisis, clinical crisis, technological crisis, facilities crisis, financial or business crisis, human resources crisis, leadership or governance crisis, natural disaster, public safety crisis, racial or identity conflict, or student affairs crisis). Recent examples include student deaths and suicides, academic and athletic scandals, cyberattacks, bomb scares, natural disasters, tensions due to race relations, and leadership and governance challenges due to public debate and disagreement with the state legislature. Recalling some of the definitions summarized in chapter 3, these events and situations could logically be classified as crises due to the threat placed on stakeholders and the reputational implications placed on the institution (Coombs, 2015; Heath & Millar, 2004; Ruff & Aziz, 2003). In many instances, these events or situations serve as turning points (Fink, 1986) for the institution—and at times, for the broader sector of American higher education—in terms of how individuals and institutions conceptualize, prepare for, and address these disruptions. Although it is easy to categorize these moments as crisis-like, it is worth revisiting Grint's (2005) claims that a crisis does not necessarily emerge objectively; rather, a situation becomes a crisis "at the point at which a 'crisis' is pronounced by someone significant and becomes accepted as such by significant others" (p. 1474). Put another way by Hay (1996), "Crisis, then, is not some objective condition or property of a system defining the contours for subsequent ideological contestation. Rather, it is subjectively perceived and hence brought into existence through narrative and discourse" (p. 255). Leaders have an opportunity to frame events communicatively as crises, but this framing depends on the receptivity, expectations, and assumptions of other stakeholders inside and outside of the organization (Ruben & Gigliotti, 2016a, 2016b). The framing of crisis, then, is jointly shaped by both leaders and followers—and as such, it is difficult to disentangle the situation from the jointly constructed framing of the situation. As Grint (2005) describes the difficulty of separating the situation from the leaders, "The former is often a consequence of the latter," noting that "in short leaders provide accounts of the world that are implicit in our understanding of 'the situation'" (p. 1490). This account is jointly shaped through communication by both the leader and the many stakeholders who have an interest in the organization and the crisis.

Adding to the complexity of the joint construction of crisis are the many stakeholders who have an interest in the work of higher education. As one chancellor noted in an interview, "I think there's a high degree of scrutiny of things that goes on in higher education, where you have a number of vested interest groups from the legislature to the governor, media, alumni, and potential employers, so all of these groups are looking at what's going on here from different lenses. A crisis can have a lot of reverberations in lots of different ways" (Participant 28). These stakeholders often have competing expectations for higher education, and as suggested by S. E. Lawrence (2017), "A significant leadership challenge results from the fact that there is often a fair amount of variance in understandings of a university/college's mission among external constituencies" (p. 56). The wide array of internal stakeholders, including students, faculty, staff, and administrators, also tend to view the institution of higher education through different lenses. Thus, what might be perceived as a crisis for one stakeholder group may not be seen as such by other stakeholders. Leaders in higher education must understand these varying, and at times competing, assumptions and expectations from the different internal and external stakeholders, while still taking seriously the perceptions of crisis from any of the groups. As another interviewee noted, "When you become a public higher education [leader], you have to manage up, down, and like thirty-two other directions. It's not just your board or your boss and your staff, it's all the other stakeholders" (Participant 1). Within the context of crisis, this challenge is frequently urgent, public, and subject to a wide degree of scrutiny. For these reasons, it is important to call attention to the framing behaviors of leaders (Fairhurst, 2007; Fairhurst & Sarr, 1996), while also attending to the critical role of stakeholder perceptions and their joint efforts in the construction of the crisis frame.

The findings from this project point to the multiple definitions of crisis, the critical role of the leader in both detecting and monitoring higher education crises, and the socially constructed nature of crisis in higher education. Again, leaders must attend to events or situations that are perceived by others as crises, and leaders also have an opportunity to offer a communicative framing of events or situations as crises for any number of reasons. Given these findings, what might this suggest about the widely invoked condition of "crisis in American higher education"? This current historical moment is marked by the convergence of numerous institutional and environmental challenges, the existence of varying and at times competing stakeholder expectations, and the availability of numerous digital platforms and media technologies through which to publicly disseminate news and scrutinize leaders in higher education. A discussion of whether crisis in American higher education is overblown must consider these three distinct, yet interdependent, variables.

Implications for Crisis Leadership

Heeding the advice for communication research to be consequential and pragmatically beneficial (Dainton & Zelley, 2019; Daly, 2000; Zelizer, 2015), the following applied takeaways emerge directly from this research study of the dynamics of crisis leadership in higher education. It is my hope that these theory-informed and research-driven implications are general enough to be useful for academic and administrative leaders of any type of college or university across the country, regardless of size, scope, and structure, while also being somewhat distinct from the typical crisis management–oriented insights put forward by other authors.

PERCEPTION MATTERS

Given that crises are perceived and defined differently by a wide array of institutional stakeholders, leaders in higher education must seriously attend to these varying perceptions from both internal and external constituent groups. Individual perceptions matter, and as socially constructed phenomena, crises exist if others perceive the existence of crisis. As suggested by Menghini (2014), "Leaders play a key role in determining when a crisis is a crisis . . . by [relying] on intuition and experience, as well as on cues about what threats the situations might pose to both their institutions and their individual ability to lead" (pp. 180, 182). It would be wise for leaders to err on the side of taking stakeholder perceptions seriously, as opposed to discarding claims of "crisis" as isolated examples of negative or unfavorable individual sentiment. Furthermore, by encouraging distributed leadership and cultivating collective awareness of stakeholder perceptions, senior leaders can invite others into this important and ongoing process of audience analysis.

INSTITUTIONAL SCOPE

The interdependent influence of crisis situations demands attention and vigilance from all senior leaders. Although there is a natural tendency to focus primarily on those crises that are most germane to one's unit or division, the findings from this project suggest that crises—as opposed to more localized incidents, problems, or difficulties—require an institutional focus and may often have a cascading impact across individual units or divisions and across institutions. Recall the comment from a vice president for Student Affairs: "I don't think about these crises as student affairs crises, I think of them just as institutional crises, and so, you know, I have a portfolio that involves some of the crises that occur, but they're really institutional crises" (Participant 21). She went on to acknowledge later in the interview that as an "institutional officer, your purview is not just your portfolio. . . . So, like when we had this racist, misogynist e-mail, that wasn't just a student affairs problem, that was a campus-wide problem" (Participant 21). By adopting an institutional lens, senior leaders in higher education can better grapple with the interdependent complexities associated with crisis situations in higher education.

Related to the previous point, the responsibilities for preparing for, managing, and responding to crisis situations in higher education often extend beyond one individual or one department. The interdependent influence of these situations calls for high-performing incident response teams or offices dedicated to institutional risk management that share primary responsibility for all aspects of the crisis event. These teams can ascertain the facts surrounding crisis situations, particularly since "in crisis, the facts are not entirely clear" (Participant 15), and subdivide the immediate and long-term tasks for moving forward based on one's primary responsibility and area of expertise. Leadership is a communicative process of social influence (Ruben et al., 2017; Ruben & Gigliotti, 2016), and as supported by the growing body of literature on distributed leadership (Bennett, Wise, Woods, & Harvey, 2003; Bolden, 2011; Gronn, 2000; Uhl-Bien, 2006), leadership and social influence in higher education are often distributed in crisis situations. As defined by Bennett et al. (2003), "Distributed leadership is not something 'done' by an individual 'to' others, or a set of individual actions through which people contribute to a group or organization." Rather, it is "a group activity that works through and within relationships, rather than individual action" (p. 3). Although one or more individuals will likely take on a dominant leadership role in shaping the actions of the team, an outcome of a high-performing team is that "you don't have to make decisions in isolation" (Participant 23). This collective approach to leadership, particularly in crisis situations, is made especially relevant given the sacrosanct tradition of shared governance in American higher education and the need for increased collaboration across academic and administrative siloes in addressing contemporary issues of shared significance.

THE COUNTERCULTURAL NEED FOR AGILITY

Colleges and universities face a noteworthy obstacle when it comes to effective crisis management, communication, and leadership, due in part to our decentralized organizational structure. The pervasive tradition of committee-based decision making and the tradition of shared governance further complicate the rapid response demanded by crisis situations. Crises require immediate attention (Laermer, 2003; Mitroff, 2004), yet there is a long-standing expectation of careful, deliberate, and democratic decision-making efforts. Colleges and universities are regularly criticized for being slow-moving operations (Krakowsky, 2008; Ruben et al., 2008); and agility may, at times, seem countercultural. Scott Cowen (2018), president emeritus of Tulane University, who led the institution through Hurricane Katrina and its aftermath, offers an important distinction between shared governance and shared decision making:

> I used to say that when Hurricane Katrina nearly destroyed Tulane University, in the fall of 2005, it was the temporary suspension of shared governance that allowed us to recover. Our renewal plan, which involved tremendous institutional restructuring in a short time, precluded the lengthy deliberations prescribed by normal governance procedures. But with the benefit of hindsight and another decade of experience in university leadership, I've come to realize that what occurred after Katrina was not, in fact,

the suspension of shared governance, but rather the emergence of a more effective and unencumbered version of shared governance.

One of the primary goals for leaders is to create a culture of preparedness that allows for agile and swift—yet also sound and thoughtful, values-based, and stakeholder-centered—decision making when crisis situations occur. Note that this need builds upon the previous items, in that it requires attention to stakeholder perceptions, demands an institutional focus, and relies very much on the collective and collaborative spirit of decision making found in higher education institutions. A more "nimble and flexible" approach to shared governance can thus become a "competitive advantage" for institutions of higher education, rather than an "impediment" that slows down response processes (Cowen, 2018).

INFRASTRUCTURE FOR USING AND MONITORING SOCIAL MEDIA ACTIVITY

Social media, and the use of digital media more broadly, emerged as a central theme in my conversations with senior institutional leaders. As discussed in chapter 3, social media contribute to the acceleration, accentuation, and elevation of events to the level of crisis. As a democratizing force, the media can be used to the advantage of institutional representatives as a way of disseminating information and helping to shape perceptions associated with crisis situations. In much the same way that social media allow for a rapid and broad dissemination of information on the institution's behalf, they may also create the conditions for the rapid and broad dissemination of undesirable information among their diverse users. In a recent feature on social media and university leadership in the *Chronicle of Higher Education*, Gardner (2016) posited the following: "When a protest begins or a racial incident is reported, a clock starts ticking. A president and his or her team must evaluate how to respond, and quickly. If they delay, the competing voices of social media can quickly take over the narrative, or it can appear that the president is insensitive or oblivious to the situation" (p. 4). Not only must leaders in higher education accept the mechanism of social media as a platform for communicating with geographically diverse stakeholder groups, but individuals must develop expertise in monitoring social media activity as it relates to crisis preparation. As one chief of staff for a chancellor put it, "We're doing as best we can, but I don't think most universities have thought about putting together a sophisticated infrastructure . . . as it relates to the rise in social media" (Participant 25). A number of organizations, such as the Council for Advancement and Support of Education, Academic Impressions, and the Social Media Strategies Summit, are now offering conferences, webinars, and white papers on how best to use and monitor social media for the benefit of higher education. Additionally, there is a quickly growing array of proprietary software that colleges and universities may purchase to help monitor and manage their social media activity, including Hootsuite, Sprout Social, Brandwatch, and NetBase, along with others. The art and science involved in detecting and monitoring crises, as offered in this book, requires a commitment of resources on behalf of university leadership.

PREPARING FOR THE INEVITABILITY OF "CRISIS"

In supporting his position for more crisis-oriented training and development for leaders in higher education, one administrator suggested: "The world gets more complicated. It doesn't get simpler. There's always going to be either evil people doing horrific things or stupid people doing stupid things or systems that are corrupt. Inevitably, yeah, you're going to confront it. It's just the sense of what's the magnitude of the challenge, but you're going to have challenges" (Participant 30). Given the ubiquity of crisis-like situations in higher education, crisis preparation is paramount. There are many linear and prescriptive strategies in the literature that one might adopt to prevent, avoid, or prepare for crisis situations (Benoit, 1995, 1997; Coombs, 2015; Fortunato, 2008; Heath & Millar, 2004; Mitroff, 2004; Sellnow & Seeger, 2013). The crisis taxonomy offered in chapter 4 may serve as a guide for designing crisis preparation efforts, ensuring that leaders in higher education consider the diversity of crisis situations that might impact their institution. Furthermore, consistent with cultivating an institutional orientation, there may be value in encouraging leaders to consider possible cases that extend across one's individual unit or division. According to a senior leader representing a division of Facilities Management, "Just plan and plan and plan and think you've planned for everything, but when the incident comes down, there's always going to be a ton of things that you didn't plan for. You almost need to plan for the worst-case scenario, always. Hopefully, when something happens it's not the worst-case scenario and you're much better prepared for it" (Participant 2). Popular approaches to crisis planning include informal and formal seminars and workshops, emergency tabletop exercises, full-scale operational exercises, crisis communication simulations, operations-based exercises, and functional exercises (Homeland Security Exercise and Evaluation Program, 2013).[1] The results from this study seem to suggest that these approaches to crisis planning, particularly those that are currently utilized by colleges and universities, are not fully adequate in dealing with the scale and scope of contemporary crisis situations.

Media training is often embedded in broader crisis preparation efforts. The ways in which senior leaders and outside media frame situations or events as crises play a critical role in shaping stakeholder perceptions. When asked to reflect on his advice following a major institutional crisis, a senior Academic Affairs leader offered the following: "Anybody who wants to be an administrator should get some very, very good media training, because it looks awful whenever you have the information, and you say, 'no comment,' or just can't answer the question, you're too scared, or you say something stupid, and it makes the situation worse. Media training is extremely valuable when the crisis hits" (Participant 4). Of the voluminous writing on best practices for communicating with the media during crisis, three principles stand out as most useful according to Coombs (2018) and others: be quick, be consistent, and be open. Related to this final principle, the following insight from Doug Lederman, coeditor of *Inside Higher Ed*, is especially critical to the notion of crisis leadership raised in this project: "I can say that in crisis, one should be honest and forthright. Don't ever try to hide the truth because if the media believe you are covering up the truth, or if it is found that there were truths being covered up, there is a good chance that will be worse than the actual crisis itself" (quoted in Parrot, 2014, p. 171). The importance of being forthcoming is a sentiment shared by Buller (2018): "It's often not the misdeed but the attempt to cover it up that does the most damage to reputations, institutions, and personal legacies" (p. 29).

The media have responsibility for making decisions about what news is covered and the tone of the coverage. Many senior leaders involved in this project acknowledged the media's role in "driving a crisis" (Participant 13), so much so that "they'll pick up on a story if it already supports an existing narrative" (Participant 5). Thus, as it relates to media training, it is not enough for leaders in higher education to gain comfort and confidence in communicating with the media. Leaders must also proactively identify ways of building and cultivating relationships of trust with media professionals, recognizing their key framing role when crisis situations occur. According to Lawson (2007), "Indeed, during a crisis, the manner in which an institution responds to media inquiries may make a real difference in how the institution's responsiveness or professionalism is portrayed to each of its target audiences and the general public" (p. 107). When facts are falsely presented in the media's report of an event or situation, leaders in higher education need to determine the best ways to correct inaccuracies using the most appropriate channels available. Given the emphasis on stakeholders throughout this project, it is worth reiterating the media's role as a critical stakeholder that deserves attention from both academic and administrative leaders in higher education.

TRAINING AND DEVELOPMENT

Building upon the previous points of careful and deliberate preparation in general, and the role of media training specifically, the findings from this project raise several important implications as it relates to training and development in higher education. Many senior leaders commented on the utility and value of their participation in formal and informal training and development initiatives related to crisis management and crisis communication, and as previously discussed, the kind of training that is needed depends on the way that one thinks about crisis and one's specific crisis responsibilities.

Additionally, there is a clear need for more thorough and deliberate preparation of leaders in higher education, particularly as it relates to the complex evolution of crisis situations. The "trial by fire" approach that many respondents identified in this project is neither sufficient nor sustainable. As leaders make the transition into roles with more extensive institution-wide responsibility, formal and informal mentoring and shadowing opportunities may be useful as individuals "see other people in crisis and how they respond to it" (Participant 8). Succession planning efforts can also be used to identify, recruit, and prepare leaders who are equipped to navigate these demanding crisis situations. Additionally, taking into consideration the constructionist approach used in this work, leadership training and development efforts could focus more directly on strategies for preventing situations from evolving into crises. By gaining a deeper understanding of the role of framing and the management of meaning in higher education leadership, leaders can treat crisis situations as ongoing phenomena that require routine attention.

Crisis situations demand a unique set of leadership competencies, skills, and values—many of which are summarized in the previous chapter and all of which might be included in the wide array of existing higher education training and development programs. Furthermore, a comprehensive leadership communication orientation may add greater nuance and depth to these existing leadership development initiatives. Rather than solely emphasizing the reputational impact of crisis situations, these initiatives have an opportunity to highlight the socially constructed and often subjective emergence of crises in higher education, prepare leaders for the multifaceted practice of crisis leadership, and equip leaders with an orientation that extends beyond their individual unit, department, or institution. Additionally, crisis situations and the corresponding leadership decisions can serve as unique examples for teaching and learning in a wide array of training and development initiatives. These findings highlight the importance of emergency planning and media training, but they also point to the need for sophisticated training in the area of higher education crisis leadership.

LEARNING FROM CRISES AND CRISIS LEADERSHIP ACROSS SECTORS

Institutions of higher education may be different from other types of organizations based on a number of characteristics, many of which have been presented throughout the book, including multiple, sometimes blurry purpose(s)/mission(s); unclear "bottom line"; structural complexity; loosely coupled elements, decentralization, and "shadow systems," whereby individual departments and units create their own structures and services (e.g., technology and accounting functions) because the central systems do not provide adequate or necessary services; distinctive internal administrative and academic units with (often vastly) different structures, cultures, accountability requirements, core values, and leadership traditions and practices; differing core values among administration, academics, staff, and students; decentralized decision making; traditions of autonomy, self-direction, academic freedom, and collegial decision making; and an absence of attention to succession and transition planning (Ruben & Gigliotti, 2017a). In many other ways, however, colleges and universities share much in common with other organizations. For example, corporations, government, nonprofits, and religiously affiliated organizations all have an extensive array of internal and external stakeholders who influence and are influenced by the activities of the organization (Ruben & Gigliotti, 2017a). Additionally, while crisis leadership competencies are reflective of position and experience, many of the competencies needed for crisis leadership are crosscutting in nature. Positional experience cuts both ways in that it can inform how one approaches future situations, but it can also limit leaders from adapting to the complexities of a changing environment (Gigliotti, 2019). Many of the principles, values, and characteristics of crisis leadership arguably extend across organizational types. Given that many similar expectations are placed on colleges and universities as they relate to the practice of crisis leadership, there is an opportunity for higher education leaders to learn from crises and responses to crises across organizational types in order to inform approaches to crisis leadership within higher education.

HIGH EXPECTATIONS; POTENTIALLY LIMITED REALITY

Despite the many similarities between institutions of higher education and other organizations, a unique variable emerged in this research that deserves mention. When situations perceived as crises occur, many will look to the senior leader for guidance, hope, and a sense of security. Many administrators whom I interviewed acknowledged the critical role of the leader in managing the meaning of these disruptive moments (Smircich & Morgan, 1982). As one interviewee shared, "The leader's job is to control as much fear, and make sure people are safe. So yes, the leader is critically important" (Participant 4). Or as another individual noted: "People want to hear from [the leader] for a whole host of reasons. Maybe they want to feel comforted and safe. Maybe they want information. Maybe it's all about hearing from that chief executive officer, because that voice at that time, indicates how important the issue is" (Participant 34). Leaders hold a great deal of responsibility for the well-being of the institution and of its stakeholders, and crisis situations heighten emotions, raise expectations, and orient internal and external audiences toward the words and actions of the leaders.

Despite the tremendous responsibility and expectations placed on leaders during crises, individual leaders or collective groups of senior leaders in higher education are somewhat limited in terms of what they can individually accomplish. As already suggested, unlike corporations and other organizations, leadership is widely distributed, decision-making remains shared among various actors and governing bodies, and change often occurs at a slow pace—all of which run to counter to the agile, nimble, and swift response to crisis that is widely expected. Consider the series of protests across the country regarding race relations and the significant demands placed on senior leaders by students and other stakeholders. Chancellors and presidents across the country certainly hold great influence and authority, yet they remain fully accountable to governing boards, they share responsibility with faculty as part of shared governance structures, and as offered throughout this project, they must weigh a diverse array of expectations across stakeholder groups. Furthermore, there is often disagreement on how best to move forward in the face of crisis situations. As Berrett and Hoover (2015) describe this tension in light of these campus racial protests, "Many institutions—some riven by protests or shamed by bigotry—are weighing lists of demands, an array of strategies for promoting inclusion. But changing a racial climate is a long-term struggle, students, faculty, and administrators agree. And nobody, anywhere, can say exactly what it would mean to win" (para. 7). As Walter Kimbrough, president of Dillard University, acknowledges in this article, "Some demands go beyond the power of even well-intentioned administrators. 'You're trying to change the entire culture of a campus . . . and I don't think any president or student affairs office can do that'" (para. 7). The reality of high expectations and limited decision making deserves further consideration as it relates to the practice of crisis leadership in higher education. Some might advocate for higher education to be run more like other organizations in order to keep up with the expectations placed on leaders during crisis situations. Other alternatives include the identification of alternative metrics for assessing leadership performance in higher education during crises, or the development and enhancement of mechanisms through which to equip these leaders with the skills for setting realistic expectations in response to stakeholder demands. I would go so far as to advocate for leaders in higher education to aspire to a higher standard in terms of ethical decision making, value-centered leadership, and dialogic communication during crisis; yet, at the same time, I do recognize the importance of acknowledging the reality of leadership limitations in higher education. Leaders in higher education face quite a paradox—at a time when institutions of higher education and their leaders should aspire to the noble role of societal standard-bearers as it relates to the practice of leadership, they face a reality of complex challenges, a decentralized system of decision making, and a culture of debate, discord, and disagreement with regard to their core purpose(s) and their future.

LET VALUES BE YOUR GUIDE

An individual's core values, along with the agreed-upon values of the department and/or institution, can guide leaders during all phases of an organizational crisis. These bold principles that we so often invoke both privately and publicly have the potential to be pushed to the periphery when crises strike. This might be the result of an excessive concern for one's reputation, or it can stem from the paralysis that one may encounter in the face of these moments that are frightening for any organization or its leaders. The desire to want to "fix" the immediate issue at hand—whether it be allegations of widespread academic fraud, the dissemination of a viral hazing video, or the backlash to follow a highly contentious on-campus speaker—can lead one to ignore or lose sight of one's individual or collective values. Of the many lessons, insights, and implications offered throughout this book, the importance of values-based leadership is arguably the most critical. These watershed moments for colleges and universities have the potential to challenge our core values, yet they also create the conditions through which these core values are made public and prominent. The use of values as a guide shifts the priority from crisis management to crisis leadership, from the management of one's reputation to the ongoing enactment of noble principles of which we are most proud.

Implications for Future Research

Future research may build upon the concepts, claims, and findings offered in this book. First, the decision to invoke the label "crisis" places certain demands and expectations on senior administrators who maintain leadership responsibility for the unit, division, and/or institution. Additional research in this area may explore the nature of social construction and the role of communication through interviews with other stakeholder groups most impacted by crisis situations, including students, faculty, staff, governing boards, and alumni, in order to better understand the similarities and differences among these groups. Future scholarship may further explore the distributed notion of crisis leadership by broadening the scope of institutions and/or the individuals beyond the senior level who are responsible for handling crisis situations. It may also be useful to compare higher education crisis types, crisis responses, and leadership behaviors and expectations with those found in other sectors, including business, nonprofits, government, health care, and religious organizations.

I identified more than 1,000 recent articles from various news outlets that characterized some type of "crisis" in higher education, yet the motivations and interests of the authors of these articles remain unclear. It may be worth interviewing or surveying these authors (or others who write about the "crisis in higher education") to assess their reasons and motivations for choosing this descriptive label. The various models and frameworks presented herein could also benefit from additional empirical research in order to further validate their adequacy and accuracy. For example, does expertise across leadership competency domains result in a quicker recovery following perceived crises; does a more dialogic approach to leadership communication result in greater trust from those most impacted by crisis situations; or do the various crisis classification schemes offered in this book capture future instances of crisis in higher education? Additionally, I continue to view crisis leadership as an act of improvisation as a promising area for future scholarship (Gigliotti, 2016). In light of the proliferation of acts of violence or athletics scandals on college and university campuses, for instance, leaders have pre-existing scripts that they are expected to follow. These scripts tend to limit communication to what I previously identified as a compliance- or reputation-focused orientation whereby leaders go through the motions, say the "right" thing, and spin the framing as a way of protecting the best interests of the individual or organization. By conducting research on crisis leadership as improvisation, future scholarship may explore the ways in which leaders "act first, think second" (Gigliotti, 2016, p. 188) despite the wealth of literature that suggests the importance of deliberate, rational, and logical decision making. Finally, further research is needed that can enhance and enrich crisis leadership training and development efforts, perhaps through a systematic investigation into the ways in which formal and informal training and development efforts prepare leaders for these multifaceted leadership roles, particularly as institutions and their leaders navigate a rapidly changing environment.

Conclusion

The communicative focus on the social construction of crisis and the theory and practice of crisis leadership in higher education will likely remain a relevant topic for colleges and universities in the foreseeable future. The multimethod investigation of this topic led to a number of rich findings for scholars and practitioners. First, there exist numerous different types of incidents or situations that are typically classified as "crises" in higher education—crises that are crosscutting in nature—organized around the following taxonomy: academic, athletics, clinical, technological, facilities, financial/business, human resources, leadership/governance, natural disaster, public safety, racial or identity conflict, and student affairs. Next, the senior leaders interviewed for this project addressed three central findings related to the process of defining and labeling phenomena as crises: there are multiple, and at times conflicting, definitions of crisis; crises are distinct from other types of events or situations; and many factors contribute to the elevation of an incident to the level of crisis, most notably the use of social media. The third set of findings captures the communicative construction of crisis in higher education. Specifically, crises are said to exist if others perceive them to exist; crises may be called into existence based on the framing of events or situations by leaders; and crisis often becomes a self-fulfilling prophecy based on one's decision to designate an event or series of events as a crisis. Finally, there are many core skills, values, and competencies associated with the practice of crisis leadership in higher education that may be cultivated through formal training and development efforts.

Given these findings, it seems important for scholars and practitioners to further interrogate the characterization and definition of crisis, the ways that leaders navigate crisis-like situations, and the communication strategies used before, during, and following crisis that extend beyond the compliance or reputation orientation that is pervasive in higher education. A more dialogic and stakeholder-centered approach to communication can help to advance colleges and universities, and their leaders, when perceived crises occur. This approach privileges the many internal and external stakeholders that are often most directly impacted by crisis-like situations. Additionally, the ideas raised in this book encourage a conceptual pivot away from more traditional reputation-oriented, formulaic, mechanistic, and prescriptive approaches to crisis management. It is my hope that these findings will contribute to an approach to viewing crisis leadership in higher education as a more robust, comprehensive, and dynamic area of study and practice—one that will likely continue to evolve as institutions of higher education, and the required skills for effective leadership, evolve to meet the needs of a rapidly changing and increasingly complex environment. The time has come for leaders across higher education to become more mindful of the communicative processes of meaning making related to crisis in higher education.

Despite the many complications and challenges that we have come to expect, it is worth concluding with a message of optimism. As noted at the outset of this volume, American colleges and universities remain widely regarded as among the finest in the world, with some going so far as to characterize this moment as higher education's "Golden Age"

(Brint, 2019). To a certain extent, these institutions are also held to a higher standard than other types of organizations based on our noble mission, aspirational vision, and laudable core values, which make many of the high-profile college and university crises detailed in this volume especially problematic. These crises often shift the national, and at times international, spotlight on these institutions of higher learning, and it is within this spotlight that leaders have an opportunity to model the principles and ideals that are most consistent with their personal values, the core values of their institution, and the values held sacred across the entire sector of higher education. To succeed in this effort, it will be increasingly important for scholars and practitioners to more seriously consider the complexity and nuance of crisis and crisis leadership in higher education and their implications for effective crisis leadership practice. The perspectives offered in this book remind us that it is truly in the darkness, chaos, and uncertainty of crisis where leadership becomes most critical, most visible, most desired.

Reflection Questions for Consideration

1. Revisit your responses to the opening questions from the conclusion of chapter 1 as you consider what you may have learned from this exploration into college and university crisis. What motivated you to read a book dealing with the topic of crisis leadership in higher education? Why is the study of this topic one of personal, professional, and/or intellectual interest? What do you hope to learn, and in what ways may you hope to enhance your own leadership skills by reading this book?

2. In what ways, if at all, has your understanding of crisis leadership in higher education evolved as a result of reading this book? Which of the quotes from the senior

leaders interviewed for this project did you find most compelling? Which of the implications for effective leadership presented in this chapter stand out as most significant to you, and what might be missing from this list?

3. In your opinion, is higher education in crisis? What advice would you share with formal, informal, or aspiring leaders in higher education as they consider ways of preparing for the inevitable crises that may lie ahead?

Acknowledgments

Many thanks to my family and friends for your encouragement and enthusiastic support throughout this journey.

Thank you to my mentor, supervisor, and dissertation chair, Brent Ruben, for the many rounds of constructive feedback that you provided on this project, and for your sincere commitment to my professional and intellectual growth.

To Laurie Lewis, Marie Radford, and John Fortunato, thank you for the detailed and encouraging feedback you provided throughout the dissertation process, all of which contributed to the insights presented in this book.

Many thanks to my current and former colleagues and teachers at Rutgers University, Villanova University, and Duquesne University for modeling many of the practices espoused in this book and for contributing in myriad ways to my personal and professional development.

My sincere thanks to Lisa Banning from Rutgers University Press for her support of the concept of this book, and to those who contributed to this book throughout its multiple stages, including Karen Verde from Green Pelican Editorial Services, Helen Wheeler from Westchester Publishing Services, Angela Miccinello from Miccinello Associates, and the anonymous reviewers.

To my colleagues in the Center for Organizational Leadership at Rutgers University, and to the participants of our various academic and administrative leadership development initiatives, for your thoughtful questions, examples, and insights that informed many of the ideas in this book.

Finally, to the senior university leaders who allowed me to interview them and share their insights in the pages ahead, thank for your time, enthusiasm, and candor. It is my hope that this project accurately reflects the themes from our conversations and that the implications and principles offered in this book are of use to the many individuals who take on these challenging, but critically important, leadership roles across institutions of higher education.

Notes

1. The Landscape of Crisis in Higher Education

1. For example, the following types of articles were not included in the final analysis: (a) articles addressing existing faculty research on national and international "crisis" or "crises"; (b) articles referring to the "Syrian refugee crisis," the "international housing crisis," or other external crises that are not connected to this project; (c) articles focusing on individual crises and personal crises (e.g., "career crisis" and "midlife crisis"); (d) articles focusing exclusively on events described as "crises" in international higher education outside of the United States (e.g., the financial crisis facing colleges and universities in Europe); and (e) articles in the *Chronicle of Higher Education* that did not explicitly address the topic of crisis in higher education, but appeared in the search because of biographical information for Goldie Blumenstyk (2014), author of *American Higher Education in Crisis? What Everyone Needs to Know.* Finally, data did not account for references to "crisis" in the comments section of the articles.

2. I conducted twenty-three interviews in person, typically at the interviewee's office location, and fourteen interviews by phone. The interviews ranged from 30 to 60 minutes, with an average time of approximately 35 minutes, resulting in more than 1,200 minutes of data.

3. I recorded the entirety of each interview with a voice recorder and uploaded the files into a password-protected folder on my computer. Using funds provided by both the Rutgers University School of Communication and Information and the Ph.D. Program in Communication, Information and Library Studies, I used professional transcription services. I carefully compared five of the transcribed interviews with the recorded interviews to ensure the reliability of the transcribed content. The interviews resulted in 575 single-spaced pages of interview data, along with nearly 50 pages of personal field notes. I identified key words, themes, and ideas in an initial reading of the transcribed data, all of which contributed to the development of a codebook. In addition to these codes, I also coded demographic information, including the type of institution (i.e., public or private), gender, and position in the institution.

Beginning first with this process of initial coding, I then engaged in subsequent phases of focused coding "using the most significant and/or frequent earlier codes to sift through large amounts of data" (Charmaz, 2006, p. 57) and then axial coding, where one creates new codes "whose purpose is to make connections between categories" (Lindlof & Taylor, 2011, p. 252). Using a constant comparative method consistent with the development of grounded theory (Glaser & Strauss, 1967), I compared the emergent categories with previous scholarship on the topic in order to generate, develop, and verify the data analysis and emergence of themes offered in this project. This interpretive process "entails not only condensing raw data into concepts but also rearranging the concepts into a logical, systematic explanatory scheme" (Corbin & Strauss, 2007, p. 56). Finally, in order to stay close to the data and account for the insights from all research participants, I analyzed both domi-nant codes and nondominant codes (Miles, Huberman, & Saldaña, 2014).

I routinely referred to the four research questions during my phase of initial coding, paying particular attention to concepts most germane to the focus of this study. Using NVivo, a qualitative data analysis (QDA) computer software package, I imported all of the transcribed interview files, imported the final codebook, and coded the qualitative data using the codes, or what are referred to as "nodes" in NVivo. The summary of coded data by code or node resulted in 338 single-spaced pages. Using a grounded theory approach, I qualitatively analyzed the coded content and categorized common themes that emerged from the data (Corbin & Strauss, 2008). Additionally, as suggested by Charmaz (2006), "As we proceed, our categories not only coalesce as we interpret the collected data but also the categories become more theoretical because we engage in successive levels of analysis" (p. 3). I elaborate throughout this volume on the emergent themes that best respond directly to my initial research questions.

Finally, in order to determine the intercoder reliability or intercoder agreement (Tinsley & Weiss, 2000) of the coding scheme, I recruited a trained graduate student to code 20 percent of the total interviews, or seven interviews. The notion of intercoder reliability refers to the degree of agreement for coding between two independent coders. Upon collectively reviewing the codebook, the other coder also used NVivo to code the qualitative interview data. NVivo also allows for the calculation of both percentage agreement and Kappa coefficient, a statistical measure that considers the amount of agreement that one might expect through chance. The coding comparison resulted in nearly 50 percent agreement among the two coders, with an increased agreement after meeting to discuss the codes following the initial coding.

2. The Social Construction of Crisis in Higher Education

1. I conducted twenty-three interviews in person, typically at the interviewee's office location, and fourteen interviews by phone. The interviews ranged from 30 to 60 minutes, with an average time of approximately 35 minutes, resulting in more than 1,200 minutes of data.

4. The Characterization and Categorization of Crises in Higher Education

1. In addition to responding to these two questions, the administrators in this study often elaborated on their understanding of what constitutes a crisis when they were asked to describe their institution's procedures for preparing for and dealing with crises on their campuses. Also, when asked to comment on past experiences with specific crises, respondents used the opportunity to detail how they distinguished the situation as unique and especially worthy of immediate attention.

5. Centrality of Communication in the Theory and Practice of Crisis Leadership

1. On July 26, 2018, an article was published in the *Chronicle of Higher Education* (Mangan, 2018) reporting on the forced resignation of the vice president of the Office of University Community, Jabar Shumate, who was hired to oversee diversity efforts in the aftermath of the SAE video.

7. Implications for Effective Crisis Leadership in Higher Education

1. See Zdziarski, Dunkel, and Rollo (2007) for a more detailed and useful exploration into crisis planning in higher education.

References

Adubato, S. (2009). *What were they thinking? Crisis communication: The good, the bad, and the totally clueless.* New Brunswick, NJ: Rutgers University Press.

Agnew, B. (2014). *Critical incidents in the tenure of higher education presidents and the competencies which define their leadership* (Unpublished doctoral dissertation). Rutgers University, New Brunswick, NJ.

Alvesson, M., & Kärreman, D. (2000). Taking the linguistic turn in organizational research. *Journal of Applied Behavioral Science, 36*(2), 1125–1149.

Alvesson, M., & Sveningsson, S. (2003). The great disappearing act: Difficulties in doing "leadership." *Leadership Quarterly, 14,* 359–381.

Arnett, R. C. (2006). Professional civility. In J. M. H. Fritz & B. L. Omdahl (Eds.), *Problematic relationships in the workplace* (pp. 233–248). New York, NY: Peter Lang.

Arnett, R. C., & Arneson, P. (1999). *Dialogic civility in a cynical age: Community, hope, and interpersonal relationships.* Albany, NY: State of University of New York Press.

Arnett, R. C., Bell McManus, L. M., & McKendree, A. G. (2013). *Conflict between persons: The origins of leadership.* Dubuque, IA: Kendall Hunt.

Ayer, A. J. (1936). *Language, truth, and logic.* New York, NY: Oxford University Press.

Barge, J. K. (2004). Reflexivity and managerial practice. *Communication Monographs, 71*(1), 70–96.

Barge, J. K. (2014). Pivotal leadership and the art of conversation. *Leadership, 10*(1), 56–78.

Barge, J. K., & Fairhurst, G. (2008). Living leadership: A systemic constructionist approach. *Leadership Quarterly, 4*(3), 227–251.

Barker, R. A. (1997). How can we train leaders if we do not know what leadership is? *Human Relations, 50,* 343–362.

Barton, L. (1993). *Crisis in organizations: Managing and communicating in the heat of chaos.* Cincinnati, OH: College Divisions South-Western.

Barton, L. (2001). *Crisis in organizations II* (2nd ed.). Cincinnati, OH: College Divisions South-Western.

Bataille, G. M., Billings, M. S., & Nellum, C. J. (2012, September). Leadership in times of crisis: "Cool head, warm heart." Washington, DC: American Council on Education.

Bataille, G. M., & Cordova, D. I. (Eds.). (2014). *Managing the unthinkable: Crisis preparation and response for campus leaders.* Sterling, VA: Stylus.

Bateson, G. (1972). *Steps to an ecology of the mind.* New York, NY: Ballantine.

Bennett, N., Wise, C., Woods, P. A., & Harvey, J. A. (2003). *Distributed leadership.* Nottingham, UK: National College of School Leadership.

Bennis, W., & Thomas, R. J. (2002). Crucibles of leadership. *Harvard Business Review.* Retrieved from https://hbr.org/2002/09/crucibles-of-leadership

Benoit, W. L. (1995). *Accounts, excuses, and apologies: A theory of image restoration.* Albany, NY: State University of New York Press.

Benoit, W. L. (1997). Image repair discourse and crisis communication. *Public Relations Review, 23*(2), 177–186.

Berger, P. L., & Luckmann, T. (1966). *The social construction of reality.* New York, NY: Doubleday Anchor.

Berrett, D., & Hoover, E. (2015, November 13). When pursuing diversity, victory is hard to define. *Chronicle of Higher Education*. Retrieved from https://www.chronicle.com/article/When -Pursuing-Diversity/234190

Birnbaum, R. (1988). *How colleges work: The cybernetics of academic organization and leadership*. San Francisco, CA: Jossey-Bass.

Birnbaum, R. (1992). *How academic leadership works: Understanding success and failure in the college presidency*. San Francisco, CA: Jossey-Bass.

Blumenstyk, G. (2014). *American higher education in crisis? What everyone needs to know*. New York, NY: Oxford University Press.

Blumer, H. (1966). *Symbolic interactionism*. Englewood Cliffs, NJ: Prentice-Hall.

Blumer, H. (2003). Symbolic interaction. In R. W. Budd & B. D. Ruben (Eds.), *Interdisciplinary approaches to human communication* (2nd ed., pp. 135–153). New Brunswick, NJ: Transaction.

Bolden, R. (2011). Distributed leadership in organizations: A review of theory and research. *International Journal of Management Review, 13*(3), 251–269.

Bolman, L. G., & Gallos, J. V. (2011). *Reframing academic leadership*. San Francisco, CA: Jossey-Bass.

Booker, L., Jr. (2014). Crisis management: Changing times for colleges. *Journal of College Admission, 222*, 16–23.

Brint, S. (2019, January 9). Is this higher education's golden age? *Chronicle Review*. Retrieved from https://www.chronicle.com /interactives/golden-age

Brown, S. (2015, November 18). At Kansas, student leaders take the blame for racial-climate concerns. *Chronicle of Higher Education*. Retrieved from http://munews.missouri.edu/daily-clip-packets /2015/11-18-15.pdf

Bruning, S. D., Dials, M., & Shirka, A. (2008). Using dialogue to build organization–public relationships, engage publics, and positively affect organizational outcomes. *Public Relations Review, 34*(1), 25–31.

Buller, J. L. (2018). *Authentic academic leadership: A values-based approach to college administration*. Lanham, MD: Rowman & Littlefield.

Calderon, V. J., & Jones, J. M. (2017, August 3). Many higher ed business chiefs fear financial future. *Gallup*. Retrieved from https://news.gallup.com/opinion/gallup/215006/higher-business -chiefs-fear-financial-future.aspx

Charmaz, K. (2006). *Constructing grounded theory* (2nd ed.). Thousand Oaks, CA: Sage.

Coombs, W. T. (2002). Assessing online issue threats: Issue contagions and their effect on issue prioritization. *Journal of Public Affairs, 2*(4), 215–229.

Coombs, W. T. (2006a). *Code red in the boardroom: Crisis management as organizational DNA*. Westport, CT: Praeger.

Coombs, W. T. (2006b). The protective powers of crisis response strategies: Managing reputational assets during a crisis. *Journal of Promotion Management, 12*, 241–259.

Coombs, W. T. (2007). Protecting organization reputations during a crisis: The development and application of situational crisis communication theory. *Corporate Reputation Review, 10*(3), 163–176.

Coombs, W. T. (2008). Campus crisis management: A comprehensive guide to planning, prevention, response, and recovery. *Journal of Higher Education, 79*(6), 724–726.

Coombs, W. T. (2015). *Ongoing crisis communication: Planning, managing, and responding* (4th ed.). Thousand Oaks, CA: Sage.

Coombs, W. T. (2018). *Ongoing crisis communication: Planning, managing, and responding* (5th ed.). Thousand Oaks, CA: Sage.

Coombs, W. T., Hazelton, V., Holladay, S. J., & Chandler, R. C. (1995). The crisis grid: Theory and application in crisis management. In L. Barton (Ed.), *Proceedings for the New Avenues in Risk and Crisis Management Conference* (Vol. 4, pp. 30–39). Las Vegas, NV: University of Las Vegas Publications.

Coombs, W. T., & Holladay, S. J. (2002). Helping crisis managers protect their reputational assets: Initial tests of the situational crisis communication theory. *Management Communication Quarterly, 16*(2), 165–186.

Coombs, W. T., & Holladay, S. J. (2005). Exploratory study of stakeholder emotions: Affect and crisis. In N. M. Ashkanasy, W. J. Zerbe, & C. E. J. Hartel (Eds.), *Research on emotion in organizations*. Vol. 1, *The effect of affect in organizational settings* (pp. 271–288). New York, NY: Elsevier.

Corbin, J., & Strauss, A. (2007). *Basics of qualitative research* (3rd ed.). Thousand Oaks, CA: Sage.

Cowen, S. S. (2018, August 13). Shared governance does not mean shared decision making. *Chronicle of Higher Education*. Retrieved from https://www.chronicle.com/article/Shared-Governance -Does-Not/244257

Craig, R. T. (2018). For a practical discipline. *Journal of Communication, 68*(2), 289–297.

Dainton, M., & Zelley, E. D. (2019). *Applying communication theory for professional life: A practical introduction*. Thousand Oaks, CA: Sage.

Daly, J. A. (2000). Colloquy: Getting older and getting better: Challenges for communication research. *Human Communication Research, 26*(2), 331–338.

Deere, S., & Addo, K. (2015, November 9). Mizzou chancellor forced out, just hours after resignation of UM president amid campus protests. Retrieved from https://www.stltoday.com/news /local/education/mizzou-chancellor-forced-out-just-hours-after -resignation-of-um/article_fa9f0aae-511c-5843-a420-fca7ce1743c6 .html

Dubois, P. L. (2006). Presidential leadership in times of crisis. In D. G. Brown (Ed.), *University presidents as moral leaders* (pp. 29–53). Westport, CT: ACE/Praeger.

DuBrin, A. J. (2013). Conclusions about crisis leadership in organizations. In A. J. DuBrin (Ed.), *Handbook of research on crisis leadership in organizations*. Northampton, MA: Edward Elgar.

Estes, C. L. (1983). Social Security: The social construction of a crisis. *Milbank Memorial Fund Quarterly: Health and Society, 61*(3), 445–461.

Factiva. (2018). Retrieved from https://global.factiva.com/

Fairhurst, G. T. (2007). *Discursive leadership: In conversation with leadership psychology.* Thousand Oaks, CA: Sage.

Fairhurst, G. T. (2009). Considering context in discursive leadership research. *Human Relations, 62*(11), 1607–1633.

Fairhurst, G. T. (2011a). *The power of framing.* San Francisco, CA: Jossey-Bass.

Fairhurst, G. T. (2011b). Leadership and the power of framing. *Leader to Leader, 2011*(61), 43–47.

Fairhurst, G. T., & Connaughton, S. L. (2014a). Leadership: A communicative perspective. *Leadership, 10*(7), 7–35.

Fairhurst, G. T., & Connaughton, S. L. (2014b). Leadership communication. In L. L. Putnam & D. K. Mumby (Eds.), *The SAGE handbook of organizational communication: Advances in theory, research, and method* (pp. 401–423). Thousand Oaks, CA: Sage.

Fairhurst, G. T., & Grant, D. (2010). The social construction of leadership: A sailing guide. *Management Communication Quarterly, 24*(2), 171–210.

Fairhurst, G. T., & Putnam, L. (2004). Organizations as discursive constructions. *Communication Theory, 14*(1), 5–26.

Fairhurst, G. T., & Sarr, R. (1996). *The art of framing: Managing the language of leadership.* San Francisco, CA: Jossey-Bass.

Fairhurst, G. T., & Uhl-Bien, M. (2012). Organizational discourse analysis (ODA): Examining leadership as a relational process. *Leadership Quarterly, 23*(6), 1043–1062.

Fingerhut, H. (2017, July 20). Republicans skeptical of colleges' impact on U.S., but most see benefits for workforce preparation. *Pew Research Center.* Retrieved from http://www.pewresearch.org/fact-tank/2017/07/20/republicans-skeptical-of

-colleges-impact-on-u-s-but-most-see-benefits-for-workforce
-preparation/

Fink, S. (1986). *Crisis management: Planning for the inevitable.* New York, NY: AMACOM.

Freeh Sporkin & Sullivan, LLP. (2012, July 12). Report of the special investigative counsel regarding the actions of the Pennsylvania State University related to the child sexual abuse committed by Gerald A. Sandusky. Retrieved from https://www .documentcloud.org/documents/396512-report-final-071212.html

Freeman, R. E. (1984). *Strategic management: A stakeholder approach.* Boston, MA: Pitman.

Fortunato, J. A. (2008). Restoring a reputation: The Duke University lacrosse scandal. *Public Relations Review, 34*(2), 116–123.

Fortunato, J. A., Gigliotti, R. A., & Ruben, B. D. (2018). Analyzing the dynamics of crisis leadership in higher education: A study of racial incidents at the University of Missouri. *Journal of Contingencies and Crisis Management, 26*(4), 510–518.

Garcia, B. D. (2015). *From crisis to stability: A case study of presidential leadership at a Christian college* (Unpublished doctoral dissertation). Western Michigan University, Kalamazoo, MI.

Gardner, L. (2016, October 9). When it comes to campus crises, college communications staffs plan, react, and fret. *Chronicle of Higher Education.* Retrieved from http://www.chronicle.com /article/When-It-Comes-to-Campus/238024

Genshaft, J. (2014). It's not the crime, it's the cover-up (and the follow-up). In G. M. Bataille & D. I. Cordova (Eds.), *Managing the unthinkable: Crisis preparation and response for campus leaders* (pp. 7–17). Sterling, VA: Stylus.

Gergen, K. (1999). *An invitation to social construction.* Thousand Oaks, CA: Sage.

Gigliotti, R. A. (2016). Leader as performer; leader as human: A post-crisis discursive construction of leadership. *Atlantic Journal of Communication, 24*(3), 185–200.

Gigliotti, R. A. (2017). *The social construction of crisis in higher education: Implications for crisis leadership theory and practice* (Unpublished doctoral dissertation). Rutgers University, New Brunswick, NJ.

Gigliotti, R. A. (Ed.). (2019). *Leadership competencies: A framework for leadership assessment, education, and research*. Bingley, UK: Emerald Group.

Gigliotti, R. A., & Fortunato, J. A. (2017). Crisis leadership: Upholding institutional values. In B. D. Ruben, R. De Lisi, & R. A. Gigliotti, *A guide for leaders in higher education: Core concepts, competencies, and tools* (pp. 299–323). Sterling, VA: Stylus.

Gigliotti, R. A., Ruben, B. D., & Goldthwaite, C. (2017). *Leadership: Communication and social influence in personal and professional settings*. Dubuque, IA: Kendall Hunt.

Gill, J. (2012). *Crisis leadership: The roles university presidents and crisis managers play in higher education—A case study of the State University System of Florida* (Unpublished doctoral dissertation). Florida International University, Miami, FL.

Glaser, B. G., & Strauss, A. L. (1967). *The discovery of grounded theory: Strategies for qualitative research*. Chicago: Aldine Publishing Company.

Gmelch, W. H. (2013). The development of academic leaders. *International Journal of Leadership and Change, 1*(1), 26–35.

Gmelch, W. H., & Buller, J. L. (2015). *Building academic leadership capacity: A guide to best practices*. San Francisco, CA: Jossey-Bass.

Gmelch, W. H., & Miskin, V. D. (2004). *Chairing an academic department*. Madison, WI: Atwood.

Grint, K. (2000). *The arts of leadership*. Oxford, UK: Oxford University Press.

Grint, K. (2005). Problems, problems, problems: The social construction of leadership. *Human Relations, 58*(11), 1467–1494.

Gronn, P. (2000). Distributed properties: A new architecture for leadership. *Educational Management Administration & Leadership, 28*(3), 317–338.

Hacking, I. (1999). *The social construction of what?* Cambridge, MA: Harvard University Press.

Hartocollis, A. (2017, July 9). Long after protests, students shun the University of Missouri. Retrieved from https://www.nytimes .com/2017/07/09/us/university-of-missouri-enrollment-protests -fallout.html?mcubz=3

Hay, C. (1996). Narrating crisis: The discursive construction of the winter of discontent. *Sociology, 30*(2), 253–277.

Heath, R. L. (1998). New communication technologies: An issues management point of view. *Public Relations Review, 24*(3), 273–288.

Heath, R. L., & Millar, D. P. (2004). A rhetorical approach to crisis communication: Management, communication processes, and strategic responses. In D. P. Millar & R. L. Heath (Eds.), *Responding to crisis: A rhetorical approach to crisis communication* (pp. 1–17). Mahwah, NJ: Lawrence Erlbaum.

Heath, R. L., & O'Hair, H. D. (Eds.). (2009). *Handbook of risk and crisis communication*. London, UK: Routledge.

Helsloot, I., Boin, A., Jacobs, B., & Comfort, L. K. (2012). *Mega-crises: Understanding the prospects, nature, characteristics, and the effects of cataclysmic events*. Springfield, IL: Charles C. Thomas.

Hermann, C. F. (1963). Some consequences of crisis which limit the viability of organizations. *Administrative Science Quarterly, 8*(1), 61–82.

Homeland Security Exercise and Evaluation Program (HSEEP). (2013). U.S. Department of Homeland Security. Retrieved from https://www.fema.gov/media-library-data/20130726-1914-25045 -8890/hseep_apr13_.pdf

Irvine, R. B., & Millar, D. P. (1998). *Crisis communication and management: How to gain and maintain control*. San Francisco, CA: International Association of Business Communicators.

Jablonski, M., McClellan, G., & Zdziarski, G. (2008). In search of safer communities: Emerging practices for student affairs in addressing campus violence. *New Directions for Student Services, 2008* (S1), 1–38.

Jacobsen, M. J. (2010). *Leadership strategies dealing with crisis as identified by administrators in higher education* (Unpublished doctoral dissertation). Texas A&M University, College Station, TX.

Johnson & Johnson. (2019). Our Credo. Retrieved from https://www.jnj.com/credo/

Jones, E., Watson, B., Gardner, J., & Gallois, C. (2004). Organizational communication: Challenges for the new century. *Journal of Communication, 54*(4), 722–750.

Kent, M. L. (2013). Using social media dialogically: Public relations role in reviving democracy. *Public Relations Review, 39*(4), 337–345.

Kent, M. L., & Taylor, M. (2002). Toward a dialogic theory of public relations. *Public Relations Review, 28*(1), 21–37.

Keohane, N. O. (2006). *Higher ground: Ethics and leadership in the modern university*. Durham, NC: Duke University Press.

Klann, G. (2003). *Crisis leadership*. Greensboro, NC: Center for Creative Leadership.

Koehn, N. (2017). *Forged in crisis: The power of courageous leadership in turbulent times*. New York, NY: Scribner.

Kolowich, S. (2015, March 28). How Sweet Briar's board decided to close the college. *Chronicle of Higher Education*. Retrieved from http://www.chronicle.com/article/How-Sweet-Briars-Board/228927

Krakowsky, R. P. (2008). *Sustaining change in higher education administrative student services* (Unpublished doctoral dissertation). Johnson & Wales University, Providence, RI.

Laermer, R. (2003). *Full frontal PR: Getting people to talk about you, your business, or your product*. Princeton, NJ: Bloomberg.

Langley, A., & Tsoukas, H. (2010) Introducing "perspectives on process organization studies." In T. Hernes and S. Maitlis (Eds.), *Process, sensemaking and organization* (pp. 1–26). Oxford, UK: Oxford University Press.

Lasch, C. (1991). *The true and only heaven: Progress and its critics.* New York, NY: W. W. Norton.

Lawrence, F. L. (2006). *Leadership in higher education: Views from the presidency.* New Brunswick, NJ: Transaction.

Lawrence, S. E. (2017). Higher education's multiple stakeholders. In B. D. Ruben, R. De Lisi, & R. A. Gigliotti (Eds.), *A guide for leaders in higher education: Core concepts, competencies, and tools* (pp. 53–66). Sterling, VA: Stylus.

Lawson, C. J. (2007). Crisis communication. In E. L. Zdziarski, N. W. Dunkel, & J. M. Rollo (Eds.), *Campus crisis management: A comprehensive guide to planning, prevention, response, and recovery.* San Francisco, CA: Jossey-Bass.

Lederman, D. (2018, July 24). Best way to contain a crisis? Practice. *Inside Higher Ed.* Retrieved from https://www.insidehighered .com/news/2018/07/24/leaders-advise-business-officers-how-best -contain-campus-crises

Leeper, K. A., & Leeper, R. V. (2006). Crisis in the college/ university relationship with the community. *Journal of Promotion Management, 12*(3), 129–142.

Len-Rios, M. E. (2010). Image repair strategies, local news portrayals, and crisis stage: A case study of Duke University's lacrosse team crisis. *International Journal of Strategic Communication, 4*(4), 267–287.

Lerbinger, O. (1997). *The crisis manager: Facing risk and responsibility.* Mahwah, NJ: Lawrence Erlbaum.

Lewis, L. K. (2011). *Organizational change: Creating change through strategic communication.* New York, NY: Wiley-Blackwell.

Li, T., & Yorke, J. A. (1975). Period three implies chaos. *American Mathematical Monthly, 82*(10), 985–992.

Lindell, M. K., Prater, C., & Perry, R. W. (2007). *Introduction to emergency management.* Hoboken, NJ: Wiley.

Lindlof, T. R., & Taylor, B. C. (2011). *Qualitative communication research methods* (3rd ed.). Thousand Oaks, CA: Sage.

Littlejohn, S. W., & Foss, K. A. (2011). *Theories of human communication* (10th ed.). Long Grove, IL: Waveland Press.

Lorenz, E. N. (1963). Deterministic nonperiodic flow. *Journal of Atmospheric Sciences, 20*(2), 130–148.

Luca, M., Rooney, P., & Smith, J. (2016). The impact of campus scandals on college applications. Working paper 16-137. *Harvard Business Review*. Retrieved from http://www.people.hbs.edu/mluca/CollegeScandals.pdf

Mangan, K. (2018, July 26). U. of Oklahoma official hired in wake of racist fraternity chant says he was forced out. *Chronicle of Higher Education*. Retrieved from https://www.chronicle.com/article/U-of-Oklahoma-Official-Hired/244057

Mann, T. (2007). Strategic and collaborative crisis management: A partnership approach to large-scale crisis. *Planning for Higher Education, 36*(1), 54–64.

Manning, K. (2012). *Organizational theory in higher education*. New York, NY: Routledge.

Marans, D., & Stewart, M. (2015). Why Missouri has become the heart of racial tension in America. *Huffington Post*. Retrieved from https://www.huffingtonpost.com/entry/ferguson-mizzou-missouri-racial-tension_us_564736e2e4b08cda3488f34d

Mead, G. H. (1934). *Mind, self, and society*. Chicago, IL: University of Chicago Press.

Menghini, R. J. (2014). *Presidential responses to crises at public university campuses: What leaders do and how others perceive their actions* (Unpublished doctoral dissertation). University of Pennsylvania, Philadelphia, PA.

Meyers, G. C., & Holusha, J. (1986). *When it hits the fan: Managing the nine crises of business*. Boston, MA: Houghton Mifflin.

Middlebrooks, A. E., Allen, S. J., McNutt, M. S., & Morrison, J. L. (2019). *Discovering leadership: Designing your success*. Thousand Oaks, CA: Sage.

Miles, M. B., Huberman, A. M., & Saldaña, J. (2014). *Qualitative data analysis: A methods sourcebook*. Thousand Oaks, CA: Sage.

Mitroff, I. I. (1994). Crisis management and environmentalism: A natural fit. *California Management Review, 36*(2), 101–113.

Mitroff, I. I. (2004). *Crisis leadership: Planning for the unthinkable.* Hoboken, NJ: Wiley.

Mitroff, I. I., & Anagnos, G. (2001). *Managing crises before they happen: What every executive and manager needs to know about crisis management.* New York, NY: AMACOM.

Mitroff, I. I., Diamond, M. A., & Alpaslan, C. M. (2006). How prepared are America's colleges and universities for major crises? Assessing the state of crisis management. Ann Arbor, MI: Society for College and University Planning. Retrieved from http://www.scup.org/page/knowledge/crisis-planning/diamong

Mitroff, I. I., Harrington, K., & Gai, E. (1996, September). Thinking about the unthinkable. *Across the Board, 33*(8), 44–48.

Mondics, C. (2017, January 7). Penn State's legal tab for Sandusky: $250 million and counting. *Philadelphia Inquirer.* Retrieved from http://www.philly.com/philly/news/20170108_Penn_State_s _legal_tab_for_Sandusky___250_million_and_counting.html

Muffet-Willett, S. L. (2010). *Waiting for a crisis: Case studies of crisis leaders in higher education* (Unpublished doctoral dissertation). University of Akron, Akron, OH.

National Center for Free Speech and Civic Engagement. (2019). Retrieved from https://freespeechcenter.universityofcalifornia .edu/

Northouse, P. G. (2018). *Leadership: Theory and practice* (8th ed). Thousand Oaks, CA: Sage.

Ohlheiser, A. (2015, March 9). With their fraternity closed, University of Oklahoma's Sigma Alpha Epsilon members move out. *Washington Post.* Retrieved from https://www .washingtonpost.com/news/grade-point/wp/2015/03/09/with -their-fraternity-closed-oklahoma-universitys-sigma-alpha -epsilon-members-move-out/?utm_term=.4e977964f0ef

Pang, A., Nasrath, B., & Chong, A. (2014). Negotiating crisis in the social media environment: Evolution of crises online, gaining credibility offline. *Corporate Communications: An International Journal, 19*(1), 96–118.

Parrot, T. V. (2014). Working effectively with the media: Advice from the front line. In G. M. Bataille & D. I. Cordova (Eds.), *Managing the unthinkable: Crisis preparation and response for campus leaders* (pp. 170–180). Sterling, VA: Stylus.

Pauchant, T. C., & Mitroff, I. I. (1992). *Transforming the crisis-prone organization: Preventing individual, organizational, and environmental tragedies.* San Francisco, CA: Jossey-Bass.

Pérez-Peña, R. (2011, November 21). Rich in success, rooted in secrecy. *New York Times.* Retrieved from https://www.nytimes.com/2011/11/22/sports/ncaafootball/penn-states-graham-spanier-enjoyed-success-and-secrecy.html

Perrow, C. (1984). *Normal accidents.* New York, NY: Basic Books.

Persuit, J. M. (2013). *Social media and integrated marketing communication.* Lanham, MD: Lexington Books.

Potter, J. (1996). *Representing reality: Discourse, rhetoric, and social construction.* Thousand Oaks, CA: Sage.

Readings, B. (1996). *The university in ruins.* Cambridge, MA: Harvard University Press.

Roitman, J. (2014). *Anti-crisis.* Durham, NC: Duke University Press.

Rollo, J. M., & Zdziarski, E. L. (2007). The impact of crisis. In E. L. Zdziarski, N. W. Dunkel, & J. M. Rollo (Eds.), *Campus crisis management: A comprehensive guide to planning, prevention, response, and recovery* (pp. 3–34). San Francisco, CA: Jossey-Bass.

Rorty, R. (1967). *The linguistic turn: Recent essays in philosophical method.* Chicago, IL: University of Chicago Press.

Rost, J. C. (1991). *Leadership for the twenty-first century.* New York, NY: Praeger.

Ruben, B. D. (2004). *Pursuing excellence in higher education: Eight fundamental challenges.* San Francisco, CA: Jossey-Bass.

Ruben, B. D. (2005). Linking communication scholarship and professional practice in colleges and universities. *Journal of Applied Communication Research, 33*(4), 294–304.

Ruben, B. D. (2006). *What leaders need to know and do*. Washington, DC: NACUBO.

Ruben, B. D. (2012). *What leaders need to know and do: A leadership competencies scorecard* (2nd ed.). Washington, DC: National Association of College and University Business Officers.

Ruben, B. D. (2016). Communication theory and health communication practice: The more things change, the more they stay the same. *Health Communication, 31*(1), 1–11.

Ruben, B. D., De Lisi, R., & Gigliotti, R. A. (2017). *A guide for leaders in higher education: Core concepts, competencies, and tools.* Sterling, VA: Stylus.

Ruben, B. D., & Gigliotti, R. A. (2016). Leadership as social influence: An expanded view of leadership communication theory and practice. *Journal of Leadership and Organizational Studies, 23*(4), 467–479.

Ruben, B. D., & Gigliotti, R. A. (2017a). Are higher education institutions and their leadership needs unique? Vertical and horizontal perspectives. *Higher Education Review, 49*(3), 27–52.

Ruben, B. D., & Gigliotti, R. A. (2017b). Communication: Sine qua non of organizational leadership theory and practice. *International Journal of Business Communication, 54*(1), 12–30.

Ruben, B. D., Lewis, L. K., Sandmeyer, L., Russ, T., Smulowitz, S., & Immordino, K. (2008). *Assessing the impact of the Spellings Commission: The message, the messenger, and the dynamics of change in higher education*. Washington, DC: National Association of College and University Business Officers.

Ruff, P., & Aziz, K. (2003). *Managing communications in a crisis.* Burlington, VT: Gower.

Schultz, F., & Raupp, J. (2010). The social construction of crises in governmental and corporate communications: An inter-organizational and inter-systemic analysis. *Public Relations Review, 36*(2), 112–119.

Schutz, A. (1970). *On phenomenology and social relations.* Chicago, IL: University of Chicago Press.

Seeger, M. W. (2018). Answering the call for scholarship: The *Journal of International Crisis and Risk Communication Research*. *Journal of International Crisis and Risk Communication Research, 1*(1), 7–10.

Seeger, M. W., & Sellnow, T. L. (2016). *Narratives of crisis: Telling stories of ruin and renewal*. Stanford, CA: Stanford University Press.

Seeger, M. W., Sellnow, T. L., & Ulmer, R. R. (2003). *Communication and organizational crisis*. Westport, CT: Praeger.

Seeger, M. W., Ulmer, R. R., Novak, J. M., & Sellnow, T. (2005). Post-crisis discourse and organizational change, failure and renewal. *Journal of Organizational Change Management, 18*(1), 78–95.

Sellnow, T. L., & Seeger, M. W. (2013). *Theorizing crisis communication*. Hoboken, NJ: Wiley Blackwell.

Sen, F., & Egelhoff, W. G. (1991). Six years and counting: Learning from crisis management at Bhopal. *Public Relations Review, 17*(1), 69–83.

Seymour, M., & Moore, S. (2000). *Effective crisis management: Worldwide principles and practice*. London, UK: Cassel.

Shotter, J. (1993). *Conversational realities: Constructing life through language*. Thousand Oaks, CA: Sage.

Shrivastava, P. (1993). Crisis theory/practice: Towards a sustainable future. *Industrial & Environmental Crisis Quarterly, 7*(1), 23–42.

Siah, J., Bansal, M., & Pang, A. (2010). New media: A new medium in escalating crises? *Corporate Communications: An International Journal, 15(2)*, 143–155.

Smircich, L., & Morgan, G. (1982). Leadership: The management of meaning. *Journal of Applied Behavioral Science, 18*(3): 257–273.

Smith, M., & Hartocollis, A. (2018, May 16). Michigan State's $500 million for Nassar victims dwarfs other settlements. *New York Times*. Retrieved from https://www.nytimes.com/2018/05/16/us/larry-nassar-michigan-state-settlement.html

Stephens, K. K., Malone, P. C., & Bailey, C. M. (2005). Communicating with stakeholders during a crisis: Evaluating message strategies. *International Journal of Business Communication, 42*(4), 390–419.

Stripling, J., & Thomason, A. (2015, March 11). Oklahoma president's swift action on racist video carries risks. *Chronicle of Higher Education*. Retrieved from http://chronicle.com/article/Oklahoma-President-s-Swift/228389/

Thayer, L. (1968). *Communication and communication systems.* Homewood, IL: Richard D. Irwin.

Thayer, L. (2003). Communication: *Sine qua non* of the behavioral sciences. In R. W. Budd & B. D. Ruben (Eds.), *Interdisciplinary approaches to human communication* (2nd ed., pp. 7–31). New Brunswick, NJ: Transaction.

Theunissen, P., & Noordin, W. N. W. (2012). Revisiting the concept "dialogue" in public relations. *Public Relations Review, 38*(1), 5–13.

Tinsley, H. E. A., & Weiss, D. J. (2000). Interrater reliability and agreement. In H.E.A. Tinsley & S. D. Brown (Eds.), *Handbook of applied multivariate statistics and mathematical modeling* (pp. 95–124). San Diego, CA: Academic Press.

Uhl-Bien, M. (2006). Relational leadership theory: Exploring the social processes of leadership and organizing. *Leadership Quarterly, 17*(6), 654–676.

Ulmer, R. R., Sellnow, T. L., & Seeger, M. W. (2018). *Effective crisis communication: Moving from crisis to opportunity* (4th ed.). Thousand Oaks, CA: Sage.

University of Oklahoma. Office of University Community. (2018). Retrieved from http://www.ou.edu/community

Watzlawick, P., Bavelas, J., & Jackson, D. (1967). *Pragmatics of human communication: A study of interactional patterns, pathologies, and paradoxes.* New York, NY: W. W. Norton.

Weick, K. E. (1979). *The social psychology of organizing.* Reading, MA: Addison-Wesley.

Weick, K. E. (1988). Enacted sensemaking in crisis situations. *Journal of Management Studies, 25*(4), 305–317.

Weick, K. E. (1995). *Sensemaking in organizations.* Thousand Oaks, CA: Sage.

Wheatley, M. (2006). *Leadership and the new science: Discovering order in a chaotic world* (3rd ed.). San Francisco, CA: Berrett-Koehler.

Witherspoon, P. D. (1997). *Communicating leadership: An organizational perspective.* Boston, MA: Allyn & Bacon.

Wittgenstein, L. (1961). *Tractatus logico-philosophicus.* London, UK: Routledge & Kegan Paul.

Zdziarski, E. L. (2006). Crisis in the context of higher education. In K. S. Harper, B. G. Paterson, & E. L. Zdziarski (Eds.), *Crisis management: Responding from the heart* (pp. 3–24). Washington, DC: NASPA.

Zdziarski, E. L., Dunkel, N. W., & Rollo, J. M. (2007). *Campus crisis management: A comprehensive guide to planning, prevention, response, and recovery.* San Francisco, CA: Jossey-Bass.

Zdziarski, E. L., Rollo, J. M., & Dunkel, N. W. (2007). The crisis matrix. In E. L. Zdziarski, N. W. Dunkel, & J. M. Rollo, *Campus crisis management: A comprehensive guide to planning, prevention, response, and recovery* (pp. 35–54). San Francisco, CA: Jossey-Bass.

Zelizer, B. (2015). Making communication theory matter. *Communication Theory, 25*(4), 410–415.

Ziering, A. (Producer), & Dick, K. (Director). (2015). *The hunting ground* [Motion picture]. United States: Weinstein Company.

Index

described, 2–7, 8–11; development, 111–113; distributed process, 3, 128; effective management, 45, 77, 119–145; ethical decision making, 139; framing of crisis, 30–31, 33, 35–38, 42, 91–92, 124, 125, 134, 135, 142; honesty, 99–100, 133; identification of crisis, 8–11, 31–32, 42; institutional scope, 127–128; integrity, 87, 114, 133; label of, 88; landscape in higher education, 1–19; learning from crisis and other sectors, 136–137, 140–141; limitations, 139; media training, 133–134; motivation, 114; perception matters, 126–127; process of social influence, 3; relationship with organizational stakeholders, 86, 90, 94, 99, 102; response to situation (*see* higher education crisis, response to); responsibilities, 61, 74, 78, 107, 128–129; role of, 137–139; subject of, 6; succession planning, 136, 137; training and development, 134–136, 142; values-centered leadership (*see* core values [institutional/leader]). *See also* crisis; higher education crisis; social construction; social media

crisis management: aim, 81; communication perspective, 11–19; field, 22, 45, 46; plans, 81–83, 136; process, 83

crisis matrix, 64

cyberattack, 4, 62, 107, 123

damage containment (phase of crisis), 26

data falsification scandal, 4, 115

De Lisi, R., 64

dialogic model (message delivery), 81

Diamond, M. A., 6, 68–69

digital media. *See* media; social media

Dillard University, 138

distributed process (conceptualization of leadership), 3, 128

DuBrin, A. J., 87

Duke University, 4, 65

Dunkel, N. W., 64, 82–83

Estes, C. L., 41, 59

Exxon Valdez oil spill, 45

Factiva (global news outlet), 8

Fairhurst, G. T., 2, 28, 30, 31, 35–36, 84, 86, 90

financial impact of crisis, 5, 53, 64, 68, 121

Fink, S., 25–26, 46–47

Florida International University, 1

Fox School of Business, Temple University, 4, 115

framing of crisis. *See* crisis leadership; social construction

Freeh Report, 27. *See also* child abuse scandal; Penn State University

free speech, right to, 62, 116, 121, 140

Gallois, C., 18

Gallos, J. V., Jr., 98

Gardner, J., 18

Gardner, Lee, 98, 130

Gaza, Israel's policies, 32

Genshaft, J., 6

Gigliotti, R. A., 64, 111

Grant, D., 30

Greek systems and racist behavior, 4

Grint, K., 30, 85–86, 92, 124

Harvard University, 4

Harvey, J. A., 128

Hay, C. 42, 126

Rooney, P., 5
Ruben, B. D., 64, 105–109, 111
Ruff, P., 46
Rutgers University, 4

SAE. *See* Sigma Alpha Epsilon
SAGE Handbook of Organizational Communication, 28
Salaita, Steven, 32
Sandusky, Jerry, 27
Sarr, R., 90
scandal, 115
school closures, 120
Schultz, F., 59
Seeger, Matthew, 13, 22, 47, 122
Sellnow, T. L., 20, 47
September 11, 2001, terrorist events, 45
sex abuse scandal, 4, 5, 31
sexist behavior, 4
sexual assault, 4, 53, 107, 115. *See also* rape crimes
Seymour, M., 22
Shumate, Jabar, 152n1
Sigma Alpha Epsilon (SAE), 97–98, 152n1
signal detection (phase of crisis), 26
Smith, J., 5
social construction: in communication process, 13–14, 90–93; crisis as self-fulfilling prophecy, 33, 38–41, 42; described, 20–21, 32–41; evolution of crisis, 21–23; framing of crisis, 30–31, 33, 35–38, 125–126; future research, 140; language of, 21, 27, 28; perception versus reality, 28–29, 33–35, 47–48, 59, 78, 137–139; relationship between philosophy and language, 28; stages of crisis, 24–28; stakeholder's role, 59, 124–126; symbolic interaction and reality, 28–32; use of term, 21–22

social influence (leadership), 3
social media: accelerating, accentuating/escalating, 54–58, 78, 130; impact on crisis, 44; inflammatory post, 62; infrastructure for using and monitoring, 57, 130–131; viral campaign, 31. *See also* media
Sprout Social, 131
stakeholder: consequences for interests, 46, 81; expectations, 96, 124; external, 9, 12, 16, 18, 21, 30–31, 40, 47–48, 52, 67, 74, 89, 120, 124–125, 136, 143; future research, 140–141; impact of crisis, 5, 12–13, 38, 50, 78, 83, 95, 123; importance of, 48; informal, 47, 74; internal, 9, 12, 16, 18, 21, 30–31, 40, 47–48, 52, 67, 74, 89, 120, 124–125, 136, 143; leader's relationship with, 86, 90, 94, 99, 102; lives threatened, 51, 53, 59, 61; perceptions, 109, 126–127, 129; primary, 52; priority over reputation, 100; role in social construction, 59; theory, 48
state legislature, 123, 125
Stewart, Potter, 59–60
student debt, 119, 120
succession planning, 135, 136
suicide, incidents of, 53–54, 55, 123
Sullivan, Teresa, 32
Sweet Briar College, 66
Syracuse University, 4

Temple University, 4, 115
Texas A&M University, 4
Thayer, L., 29
Title IX, 107: violations, 4
Tulane University, 129–130
Twitter, 32
2008 financial crisis, 45
Tylenol poisonings, 45, 96–97

Ulmer, R. R., 22, 45, 46, 47
University of California, Berkeley, 116
University of Illinois at Urbana-
   Champaign, 32
University of Iowa, 1
University of Kansas, 67
University of Maryland, 4
University of Missouri, 4, 5, 24–25,
   27, 34–35
University of Montana, 4
University of North Carolina at
   Chapel Hill, 4, 115
University of Oklahoma, 4, 97–98,
   152n1
University of Puerto Rico, 121
University of Southern California,
   115
University of Virginia, 1, 4, 32
USA Gymnastics, 4
U.S. Department of Education, 4
U.S. News and World Report national
   rankings, 4, 115

values-centered leadership. *See* core
   values (institutional/leader)
vertical competencies, 105–108,
   117
violence, acts of, 4, 62, 121, 141
Virginia Tech, 20

Wall Street Journal, 8, 65
Watson, B., 18
Weick, K. E., 24, 35
Wellesley College, 65
white nationalist rally, 1, 4
Wise, C., 128
Witherspoon, P. D., 86
Wolfe, Timothy M., 24–25, 27
Woods, P. A., 128

Yale University, 4
Yiannopoulous, Milo, 116

Zdziarski, E. L., 5, 48, 64,
   82–83

About the Author

RALPH A. GIGLIOTTI, PHD, is the director of leadership development and research in the Rutgers University Center for Organizational Leadership, where he oversees a portfolio of faculty and staff leadership development initiatives and leads research efforts focused on leadership, communication, and crisis in higher education. Ralph teaches in the Department of Communication and the PhD Program in Higher Education at Rutgers. He is the coauthor of *A Guide for Leaders in Higher Education: Core Concepts, Competencies, and Tools* (2017) and *Leadership: Communication and Social Influence in Personal and Professional Contexts* (2017).

Printed in the United States
By Bookmasters